The Literacy Leader's Toolkit

Raising standards across the curriculum: 11–19

by Graham Tyrer and Patrick Taylor

D1157335

B L O O M ⌐ ⌐ ⌐

LONDON • NEW DELHI • NEW YORK • SYDNEY

Published 2013 by Bloomsbury Education
Bloomsbury Publishing plc
50 Bedford Square, London, WC1B 3DP

www.bloomsbury.com

978-1-4411-3883-5

3 5 7 9 10 8 6 4

Typeset by Fakenham Prepress Solutions, Fakenham, Norfolk, NR2 8NN
Printed and bound by CPI Group (UK) Ltd, Croydon, CR0 4YY

This book is produced using paper that is made from wood grown in
managed, sustainable forests. It is natural, renewable and recyclable.
The logging and manufacturing processes conform to the environmental
regulations of the country of origin.

Online resources accompany this book at:
www.bloomsbury.com/the-literacy-leaders-toolkit-9781441138835

Please type the URL into your web browser and follow the instructions to access
the resources. If you experience any problems, please contact Bloomsbury at:
companionwebsite@bloomsbury.com

Contents

3   The Sustaining Stage   154

4   Evaluating Impact   196

Foreword

As Samuel Taylor Coleridge rather aggressively put it 'Language is the armory of the human mind and at once contains the trophies of its past and the weapons of its future conquests'. More appealingly we all know there exists a mental form of slavery as real as any economic form and that literacy is an essential foundation of education, which is the key to eliminating that slavery. You can't argue a case which is just without a competence in language and it can truly claim to be the prerequisite of individual freedom as well as democracy and social justice. So it matters.

Here is a book which, at just the right moment for schools, attempts to provide a practical guide to making literacy a whole-school priority, not simply the task of the English Department. As the authors point out in their preface, all primary teachers have always seen it as their job to teach English. Yet in secondary schools the teachers' very love of their own subject sometimes gets in the way of their reinforcing the lead provided by specialist colleagues.

Simple things can sometimes get a school started. I came across one school recently that was having fun each week with what they called the 'dirty dozen' – 12 words most frequently and annoyingly misspelt the previous week and which the staff then share and then make a point of spelling correctly in lessons with a prize given at assembly following a draw from those pupils who spotted the correct 12. At another school, on each tutor's classroom door, is the name of the book which has mattered to them most in life and explaining the reason why. Another school shares, department by department, the task on a Friday of proposing three words which every teacher promises to use and define in each lesson in the following week with three more of their own thrown in for luck. Again it culminated with Year assemblies and the compilation of a school-created book 'Language for Thinking and Learning'.

You will find plenty even better strategies than these in this book, impressively planned and created even as the authors were carrying out their mission of working in their own school to effect a transformation. In doing so like all teachers and leaders in great schools they visited others to compare practice and find examples which they could adapt to their own context. In that process they have collected all sorts of ideas and a coherent framework which will resonate with all those in secondary schools at this time. I know from my continued involvement with many secondary schools that its publication is timely.

Personally, I am a fan of small, practical ideas many of which don't require too much effort but which in the right context can have high impact. You will find plenty here.

This book, however, has three unusual dimensions which those working on school improvement often overlook, namely, staff development; student involvement; and enlisting parents. It is worth reading on for this alone but when you link it to the vital issue of literacy you have a practical work of reference to which you will return on many future occasions.

Tim Brighouse

Introduction

Literacy launches spacecraft, because you can't build the Cassini-Huygens probe or Titan booster rockets without the registers of explanation, persuasion and technical vocabulary of nanotechnology. Words start and solve wars. Language, finely wrought, can bring peace and equity. Poetry and drama bring to life and enrich emotions and relationships; with it we can nuance and make sense of who we are and what we might become. The more complex and fine the craft of our words become, the more it is likely that we can live in a world with justice, fairness and peace.

So, it was with this passion that we embarked on our whole school literacy project in 2008. Our aim was to try to connect language and thinking. We used such tools as Bloom's taxonomy to ensure students had the language to describe, make, invent, aspire and dream. We allowed students to explore every genre of text that can make today's extraordinary, tomorrow's ordinary. We allowed them to explore books, with joy, with pleasure, free from the old days of 'read this, and then we'll test you and measure you'. A book, an mp3, a podcast, a blog, and vlog: these are possibilities for each child to see and understand where they are, and to invent where they might be.

Our mission was to encourage talking and listening, and to develop skills of interdependence, debate and innovation. Young people are alive with invention and compassion and energy. Their talk is vibrant, assertive and often expresses their confusion with their endlessly complex lives. So we were ambitious for them and expected them to be able to talk poetry, science and justice. We were wary of the potential sterility of functionality: we didn't want simply to stop there. We encouraged our students to question, imagine and create with their words. We wanted them to help shape a new Renaissance of entrepreneurial art, technology and science. We wanted them to be able to talk into existence, with others, new plays, poems, nanoprocessors, hyperdrives, wells of pure water in empty deserts and to make obsolete the language of hate and discrimination.

With 50 years' experience of teaching English between us, experience of school leadership and inspecting primary and secondary schools as an Ofsted additional inspector, we set out to explore new ways of promoting literacy.

To help us plan we looked for books or resources that would set out very clear strategies for secondary school teachers. We wanted something clear, brief and practical.

We found materials to support work in primary schools; we found academic texts about theory; and of course we had all the National Strategy resources on our shelves. But there were no 'How to' handbooks, no off-the-peg guides for literacy activists. We knew from the conferences we had attended and the talks we had given that we were not alone in our aspirations, but no such books existed. So we set out on our journey to improve the literacy standards in our school.

When Graham got to Chenderit School, there was a willingness to focus on literacy, partly because it is so closely allied to learning but also because staff were genuinely frustrated with the lack of basic literacy skills evident in their students' writing. In brief, we went through collective work trawl, presentation of evidence, reassurance that the literacy project need not involve an insurmountable contribution from hard-pressed staff and above all, a commitment to the co-construction of our cross-curricular resources with student literacy leaders.

We worked with four quite different schools. Many others have taken and used the methods described in the book when we have presented them at national conferences.

With humility but also for your reassurance, here's some evidence that we achieved success over the four years of our project:

- *93% expected levels of progress in English from 75%*
- *92% English A*–C from 65%*
- *70% whole school A*ACEM from 57%*
- *TES Outstanding Literacy Award*
- *SSAT Outstanding Literacy Award*
- *Ofsted Best Literacy Practice*
- *Ofsted school rating: Outstanding*

Now that we have achieved success, we thought it was time to write that missing practical 'How to' book based on our experiences.

Our book sets out to help every teacher sense themselves as teachers of words. Every aspect of every source of knowledge is crafted in language. We hope all our schools' classrooms celebrate, take risks and invent ways of speaking, listening and writing. Words are precious, vulnerable and robust. We must help all teachers to lead language learning with their students. Language doesn't stop at the door of the English classroom; it must be treasured and exemplified and experimented with in every part of the school and given as much status as so-called subject content, most of which, if we are honest, will be ossified within a year or two.

If there must be assessment, let's keep it simple; we believe accuracy and flair should be prioritised in equal measure. It does not matter who you are and what your background is, young people, their families and their schools are capable of the most astonishing insights and sensitivities. And to do that, no child should be allowed to drift through the system without being able to enjoy and feel confident with the core basic standards.

We want all students to become experts in the discourses of learning, to be able to talk about, debate and invent new ways of becoming exceptional electricians, poets, plumbers, space explorers and medics. We become skilled at skills when we learn how to learn, when we enjoy learning, when we feel ourselves becoming leaders and inventors of learning.

In our whole-school literacy project, we tried to open students' minds to texts they may never have heard of, to give them the freedom to choose texts that excited them, instead of dragging them through a programme of medicinal reading. We think it is important to let students see why some writers have gained status and others have not, to give them the choice as to what they want to use to make change and to be the poets and innovators of tomorrow. Of course, they should not be allowed to journey past writing of the most extraordinary influence and beauty: but force-march them and they will resent the very names of Shakespeare, Keats, Hardy, Pullman and Morpurgo. They should know what's there, and then, be able to trust their teachers to decide how to make the reading experience one of pleasure and engagement and excitement, rather than a passive, resentful gazing at a mountain of so-called literary heritage. We have so many diverse communities: if we simply compel children to read what we personally value, we risk repelling them into illiteracy.

Our literacy project tried to make the acquisition of skills personal, not linked to age. We wanted to allow students to accelerate through the craft of reading and writing and speaking at a pace that excites and liberates them.

We have ensured that our school has enough teachers of English for all of the above to happen, which does mean tough prioritisation of resources. Do students take too many subjects? Of course they do. In most schools, students are taught language skills in classes of more than 25 for just three hours a week. And then we wonder why so many of them emerge unable to use a capital letter properly at 16. If language is important, we need to expand the time they study, invent, refine and grow their skills. We believe that for at least one hour a day students should be learning and developing their language in secondary schools. You only develop in skill by constantly and enthusiastically revisiting basic knowledge, so that you grow your language talents with frequency, vibrancy and security.

We want all children to be whomsoever they wish. Only if they are excited and skilled in the arts of language will they be able to invent a future they deserve. So, it is up to us, as teachers and school leaders, to describe rather than prescribe. The language of innovation is the language of freedom.

There has never been a better time to work with our colleagues on improving literacy across the school. More and more staff are convinced that it helps students achieve the grades they need if literacy is of the highest standard. Increasingly, staff see this as a collaborative enterprise and not the sole responsibility of the English department.

We continue to use the strategies we present here successfully in our school, and they have also been used in schools in urban Warwickshire, urban Coventry and rural Northamptonshire. We also reference, for example, and with their permission, comprehensive schools in Stanmore, London; Tottenham, London; and inner city Manchester. We hope this gives you confidence that what we offer may help you wherever you are. We would like to thank the following colleagues who have worked with us on the strategies in this book:

Gaye Kassir, Park High School, Stanmore, Essex

Isabelle Valade, Trinity High School, Manchester

Natali Kojik, Park View School, Haringey.

Graham Tyrer and Patrick Taylor

How to use this book

This book is a handbook of the activities we used to raise standards in literacy in our school by implementing a whole school literacy programme.

The book can be used in a variety of ways. It can be used by a literacy coordinator to implement a whole school literacy programme over a two-year period; it can be used to implement a shorter literacy programme for a school testing the water before embarking on a brand new whole school policy; it can also be dipped into by a literacy coordinator, head of year, head teacher or classroom teacher simply looking for one-off activities to improve literacy standards.

In Part 2 of the book, we have grouped the 52 strategies into five sections:

1 Beginning stage: *how to start*

2 Embedding stage: *how to build enthusiasm*

3 Sustaining stage: *how to make literacy a day-to-day necessity*

4 Evaluating impact: *how to reflect impact to school leaders, students and parents*

5 Working with others: *how to work with other schools.*

You can choose to complete all of the strategies in this order, or pick a few from each stage; you might want to follow the links at the end of each strategy to follow a particular theme or set of ideas.

Alternatively, in Part 1 of the book, we offer advice for creating your own two-year whole-school literacy programme from scratch. This is the method we advocate and encourage the most if you are serious about improving literacy standards in your school once and for all. As well as identifying the issues you need to address before getting started (from our experience) we also provide a detailed example of a successful two-year plan, using combinations of the strategies detailed in Part 2. It's been ratifying to get feedback from many schools throughout England and Wales, that these strategies can be effective. Especially pleasing was to be asked by Ofsted to be an exemplar of best practice.

The format of the strategies

Each strategy is laid out in the same way to help you put it into practice easily, with tips and advice for planning, organisation and troubleshooting. A description of each feature included is below:

- *Literacy outcomes:* The key improvements to literacy standards that will come from the strategy.
- *Getting started:* Things to think about before getting started and details of what you need to do in preparation.
- *Putting it into practice*: Step by step instructions for putting the strategy into practice.
- *Taking it further:* Ideas for developing and extending the strategy.
- *What the staff/students say:* This book has been written for and by staff that lead literacy and those who teach it as part of their subject content. As a result we have built up a lot of feedback over the years. We have included, wherever possible, the voices of practitioners and students to encourage you that the time and effort is worthwhile. We hope you will adapt whatever you read here for your own context.
- *Links to other strategies:* Links to other strategies in the book that complement the proceeding one.

Online resources also accompany this book (see page ii for instructions on how to access them). They are a collection of material for you to adopt or adapt according to your school circumstances. They range from practical classroom resources and whole-school work trawl to monitoring and evaluation materials referred to in the book.

PART 1

Planning your Literacy Programme

Why literacy?

Not long ago some commentators prophesied the end of the written word, as computing technologies rendered traditional communication obsolete. Changes in the way we record and transmit information take place with increasing rapidity, but the precise impact of new technology on literacy is hard to predict. While we see news headlines indicating that teaching keyboard skills may supplant the teaching of cursive handwriting in some schools in the US,[1] far more often we hear of the increasing need for greater accuracy in spelling, punctuation and grammar. Organisations such as the Confederation of British Industry (CBI) regularly warn that employers have to invest in remedial literacy lessons for their staff.[2]

The importance of good writing is stressed in some surprising places. One professor of biology argues that, 'Writing, and writing well, is the key to success in many university science courses and vital in any job,' before pointing out that, 'When I mark tutorial essays today, most of my comments focus on the quality of the writing.'[3]

Rather than killing off the written word, computing and the internet have raised our expectations of reading and writing. Anyone with an internet connection has access to a library of text that would have been unimaginably large as recently as the year 2000. Because we can word-process and amend we expect our text to be well shaped and free from errors. A greater proportion of work in developed economies relies on our ability to process information.

And despite the claims of pessimists that standards are slipping, one businessman has identified ways in which we have become more critical of errors

---

[1] Indiana latest US state to drop handwriting requirement – BBC news 12th July 2011
[2] Spelling Mistakes 'cost millions' in lost online sales – BBC news 20th July 2011
[3] 'An animal-behaviour expert says schools' failure to prepare pupils for university has left them lacking basic skills,' Professor Tim Birkhead, TES February 2009

in spelling, punctuation and grammar: he claims that customer spending on a website can be cut in half by a spelling mistake, as consumers can have concerns about a website's credibility.[4]

As we all become members of knowledge-based and information-rich economies, greater opportunities will arise for those who can access and process ideas and data: that is to say, those whose skills are most advanced in speaking, reading and writing.

Literacy in the secondary school

An item on our agenda, 'Literacy across the curriculum', or 'Language across the curriculum' has a long history. In 1921, primary teacher and English inspector George Sampson famously wrote:

> Every teacher is a teacher *of* English because every teacher is a teacher *in* English. We cannot give a lesson in any subject without helping or neglecting the English of our pupils.[5]

And in 1975, the Bullock Report, *A Language for Life*, asserted the centrality of literacy and included in its recommendations that:

> Each school should have an organised policy for language across the curriculum, establishing every teacher's involvement in language and reading development throughout the years of schooling.[6]

The most significant, systematic attempt at promoting language across the curriculum in English schools was the National Literacy Strategy, which introduced the literacy hour to all primary schools in 1998.[7] Whether or not it achieved the improvement in literacy the government hoped for, the strategy did impact on the teaching of English in the classroom, in ways that could still be seen ten years after its introduction.

The Key Stage 3 strategy provided secondary schools a wide array of demands and challenges, and folders of resources identifying ways of improving literacy

---

[4] Professor Tim Birkhead, TES February 2009
[5] *English for the English*, George Sampson, Cambridge 1921
[6] The Bullock Report, *A Language for Life*, London 1975
[7] The National Literacy Strategy, DfEE 1998

across the curriculum.[8] Unfortunately, probably because these resources were so detailed and thorough, and demands on teachers' time so great, even schools enthusiastic about tackling language across the curriculum did not secure the progress their authors presumably intended. In fact, their greatest legacy may have been even less positive, as one head teacher observed:

> If you want a sure way to provoke a collective groan in your staffroom, announce that you are intending to hold a training day devoted to whole-school literacy. 'We did that five years ago,' someone will shout, harking back to the day the National Strategies juggernaut rolled into town with its panoply of methods.[9]

So how can we achieve what we are striving for – raised standards of literacy and language in the secondary school – efficiently and effectively, engaging rather than alienating our colleagues?

[8] Literacy and learning, Key Stage 3, National Strategy, DfES 2004
[9] Comment published in *The TES* on 5th March 2010

How to develop literacy across the curriculum

Due to a combination of many factors, creating a coherent cross-curricular strategy is a difficult task. Secondary schools are complex organisations, where many different factors affect the quality of education students receive. In terms of effectiveness, a great deal of research evidence suggests that there is more variation within a single secondary school than there is between different schools; put simply, some teams are more effective than others, and ways in which different teachers are able to deliver common expectations varies tremendously across a large staff. When we set out to devise a strategy, do we assume that our school is like a naval convoy and that we should travel at the speed of the slowest boat?

Consistency in anything can be difficult to achieve: we need only ask students to find out that they experience difference on a daily basis, some of which they enjoy; part of the pleasure of moving from a small primary school to what seems to be a large secondary school lies in the variety of different lessons, different staff and learning experiences. Subject specialists have different priorities, and often feel they have less time than they need in which to teach their own subjects; adding other responsibilities can seem like asking them to take on an enormous burden. Often, teachers feel a stronger loyalty to the goals of their own team than they do to whole-school plan.

Teachers who have been given the responsibility of coordinating cross-curricular literacy are sometimes overwhelmed by the size of the task, even when they are excited by the opportunities. From the moment they take on the challenge they need to become an advocate or enthusiast, a monitor and an evaluator, a champion and coordinator. How is it possible to combine these roles?

Our experience suggests it is important to consider and solve these issues before embarking on your literacy programme, and the following are some things you should take into consideration before getting started.

A child's performance in literacy at any one time is a consequence of a wide range of factors and experiences

Many writers on education have referred to the Nigerian proverb 'It takes a village to educate a child.' In this case, the cliché proves true: our students learn literacy first from their parents, before schooling and socialising outside the home take over. When a student in school speaks or writes a phrase in a non-standard English form, such as 'we was', consciously or unconsciously they are reacting to a range of experiences over time: how they were spoken to when younger, how they have been taught formally, how they see the task they are engaged in, how they see themselves. And the same applies to everything they say or write: whether they take care and show commitment, whether they spell correctly or write imaginatively, whether they read for pleasure or not.

Your task is not to wrestle with the sociology or linguistics that lies behind the decision to use language in one way or another, but is the purely pragmatic one of saying, 'How do we enable students to have the power to use language as effectively as they can, in every part of their school life and beyond?'

Since there are so many influences at work, we believe it is helpful to think about the child as at the heart of the 'literacy village'. You need to enlist the support of as many constituents of the village as possible. You need to ensure that every part of the school experience supports the development of high quality literacy: teachers, students, parents, governors, partner primary schools, and other organisations you work with.

From the very outset of our project our vision for the future has been as follows: students who have been through our school and are now parents, value literacy and know the importance of reading with their children. Those who attend nursery or pre-school provision happen to meet some of our older students who are visiting on work experience or carrying out a research project into language development in young children. In our vision, our primary schools work effectively as a cluster and with us, sharing high expectations, helping train our secondary teachers in aspects of language development and working with us on transition. We share information well, and pupils use the same virtual learning environment and Litweb. Our local libraries, less well-funded than they used to be, collaborate with all the local schools in promoting literacy. Our students are ambassadors for literacy, helping one another, working with their parents, some of whom work with us in school to support those who have less help at home.

For maximum impact you need to work on many things at the same time, though not necessarily with the same intensity

Changing habits is a slow business; as we hinted above, waiting for the slowest boat in our convoy to complete the voyage may mean we end up waiting a long time. If you can create momentum and develop a culture in which everyone realises that his or her role, though small, is significant, you will see unexpected benefits and effective connections.

The number of tasks you embark on will depend on the number of key staff you have to lead and the time you have available. Bearing in mind there is never enough time, you need to list the possible actions you could take on the basis of which you believe will have the greatest impact. However, if teachers are enthusiastic and willing to take on tasks which will enrich the life of the school in terms of literacy, by all means encourage them to innovate; the effect of these things is cumulative.

As long as you clarify the goals and direction you wish to move in, teachers and students will innovate and your project will gain a momentum you did not expect

Many schools have a rich culture of literary and linguistic activities: school plays, public speaking, magazines and journals, libraries. These are a fabulous part of the literacy village; they promote a love of language and literature. Once cross-curricular literacy takes hold their impact will be all the greater as pupils and teachers realise explicitly what they have always felt to be true: these activities help students develop as effective users of language. For example, you will start to see students making the link between the debates they are staging, and the development of their logical reasoning in their scientific writing.

Many of the directions we have taken have been prompted by suggestions and comments from students. We held a literacy conference and invited students and teachers from other schools across the country to attend, following a comment from students who had spoken in London and York at conferences organised by the National Literacy Trust. Two years into our project a group of students approached the head and asked if they might develop a literacy app, with blueprints and suggestions of how it might be done.

Most colleagues are willing but daunted by the scale of what they might be asked to do

Two responses recur frequently at our meetings, usually from teachers of subjects other than English: 'We are sure what you are saying is right, but we lack confidence in our own knowledge of literacy', and 'We would love to be involved, but we don't have the time.'

Part of our solution to these problems is to put the students at the centre of what we do. The students are the ones who travel between different subjects and experience literature across the curriculum. It is they who need the solutions, the transferable skills, and, we believe, the ability to make conscious choices about how they will use language. If you can involve them in designing the resources they can use to support their literacy, if you can get them to become active users of literacy skills in each of their lessons, much of the responsibility will shift away from the teacher.

However, you do need teachers to engage with the material and the subject, because if they are more confident users of literacy skills they will plan for it and use it in their teaching. Therefore you need to devote a lot of energy to training; we built it into our twice-weekly staff briefings and recommend that you do something similarly frequent.

You need to remind yourselves constantly that every step you take is progress that did not exist before, and is a little victory

During your monitoring and evaluation you will constantly turn up evidence of students you have not yet reached, or teachers who have not yet embraced the possibilities of their roles. These teachers need to be challenged and supported, but you do not need to let your unflinching focus detract from the successes. Each student who gains in confidence and accuracy has enhanced their ability to succeed in a wide range of activities once they leave school; with luck they will turn out to be a literate parent, and in turn a useful contributor to the literacy village.

A final word of advice

When we were getting started on our literacy programme, we knew that we needed to get our staff to embrace the literacy imperative and we needed to quickly overcome the inevitable stumbling block of colleagues feeling overburdened when we expected them to add to their core content.

So, how do you make the literacy programme easy to manage and incorporate it into a whole-school policy?

As our previous work and experience was based on practical ideas for use in secondary schools we built on what we already knew. In previous schools we had involved parents in supporting literacy and trained students as leaders.[10] We knew that any one child's achievement in any area of learning was the product of many different factors. So we decided to set as our goal: 'Building a literacy community', getting as many people as we could involved in supporting high quality speaking and listening, reading and writing. Creating the literacy village.

We kept telling ourselves to keep focused on key improvement areas like the use of connectives, internal punctuation and extended writing. We encouraged one another to be patient, persistent and share strategies that get results. Hence, in this book we want to contribute, with humility and excitement, from our experience to your literacy project. The prize of seeking, finding and maintaining an exceptionally literate community is more important than any other.

The key to our programme is student involvement. They are the ones who move between lessons; it is inside their heads that we want the connections to be built, not in policy documentation and minutes of meetings.

In our school we worked alongside students; they are our activists and advocates. Still today, when colleagues come to visit us or when we speak at conferences our students come too, in person or on film. This is why, in this book, we offer strategies that require students to take a lead. This is also pedagogically sound. There is plenty of evidence that, when students are involved in peer teaching and peer assessment, there is an improvement in the likelihood of standards gains. (See the end of this section for further reading on this.)

As well as getting students involved, another point that needs stressing from the outset is the importance of time. We found it important, despite the pressures and imperatives within which you work, that you do not expect instant successes. If you are just starting seriously to raise the profile of literacy in your school, give yourself 24 months. At about this point you will have enough standards evidence

---

[10] *Learning to Lead*, Graham Tyrer, Continuum, London 2010

to know whether what you have tried is effective. We have learned to be persistently patient and you should do the same. Often in schools, there seems to be an inclination towards designing and implementing very quick fixes. We think it is important to resist this and put in the time and work to set up a whole-school literacy programme, using a two-year strategy, which we go into in more detail later on.

Saying this, one can claim significant standards gains by, for example, 'hothousing' a small group of students by extracting them from the timetable and tackling nothing but literacy. However, these sets of approaches are unlikely to enlist the support of colleagues, because they cannot connect the intensiveness of this approach with their curriculum planning. It is more effective to engage staff using focus, simplicity and evidence.

That's not to say that there aren't important interventions that need to take place if, say, a child arrives at the secondary phase with a reading age six months or more behind their chronological age. These students need urgent intervention that balances the literacy needs of these students with their access and connection to the curriculum content being taught to their peers.

After and before school, tutor times, and English lessons are valuable times when these students' provision will be least disrupted and their literacy standards raised. We must not let such students stagnate in whole-class settings, merely hoping that differentiation and the necessarily limited support by in-class teaching assistants can help improve their skills.

We hope that you will use the book in whatever way suits you. Feel free to try, adopt or adapt any strategy that seems to have standalone value. We recommend the whole school two-year approach, for which we provide a detailed example, but you might wish to start by just trying the 'Beginning stage' strategies from Part 2 of this book, especially if the role of literacy leader is new to you. What we are offering is a range of strategies we know work. You must choose those that best suit your circumstances.

Further reading

Ploetzner R., Dillenbourg P., Praier M. & Traum D. (1999) 'Learning by explaining to oneself and to others'. In P. Dillenbourg (ed.) *Collaborative-learning: Cognitive and Computational Approaches*. (pp. 103–21). Oxford: Elsevier.

Bruner, J.S. (1982) 'The organisation of action and the nature of adult-infant transaction'. In *The Analysis of Action*. Cambridge: Cambridge University Press.

Cheyne A. and Tarulli D. (1996) *Dialogue, Difference, and the "Third Voice" in the Zone of Proximal Development*. Retrieved April 30, 2008.

Cole, M. and Wersch J. (1994) 'Beyond The Individual-Social Antimony.' In *Discussions on Piaget And Vygotsky.* Retrieved April 30, 2008.

Cole, M. (1996) *Cultural Psychology: A Once and Future Discipline.* Cambridge: Belknap Press.

Gielen, U.P. and Jeshmaridian S. (1999) 'Lev S. Vygotsky: The man and the era.' In *International Journal of Group Tensions.* Volume 28, Numbers 314, p. 273–301.

Mooney, C.G. (2000) *Theories of Childhood: An Introduction to Dewey, Montessori, Erickson, Piaget & Vygotsky.* http://www.newworldencyclopedia.org/entry/Special:BookSources/188483485X

Schütz, R. (2004) *Vygotsky & Language Acquisition.* Retrieved April 30, 2008.

Hattie, J.A. (2008). *Visible Learning: A Synthesis of Over 800 Meta-Analyses Relating to Achievement.*

Watkins, C. (2010) 'Learning, Performance and Improvement', *Institute of Education International Network for School Improvement* Research Matters Series, No. 34.

Watkins, C. (2009) 'Collaborative learning', *School Leadership Today* 1 (1), 22–5.

Watkins, C. (2009) 'Learner-driven learning', *School Leadership Today* 1 (2), 28–31.

Mapping out a two-year plan

As previously mentioned, we believe the best chance you have for developing a whole-school strategy is implementing a two-year plan. As with any whole-school strategy it is important that a cross-curricular literacy strategy has the complete support of the head and leadership team, and, to be successful, the strategy should fit into the whole-school improvement drive. As we have suggested, many different strands and approaches can be woven into the school planning and development cycle.

In this section we have given an outline of an approach that could be used to produce a literacy programme, which we have loosely linked to a school calendar. This is based on what has been found to work in different schools. Our intention is that it gives you starting point to begin thinking about your own two-year plan. It is a description rather than a prescription.

Setting goals and direction

The head and leadership team should agree their goals and describe, in general, how they will fit into the whole-school priorities. At this stage we suggest plans should be general; they can be more carefully spelled out as part of the school development plan once some of the initial research has taken place.

It is useful to agree key ideas. For example, three fundamental principles underlined our approach:

- Literacy is fundamental to every lesson: every time a student writes, reads, speaks or listens they are potentially developing good skills and habits which will have a lifelong impact.
- Students will most effectively gain independent skills when they are invited to lead their own learning.

- Students bring with them a range of skills and experiences from their primary schools, of which secondary teachers are often unaware.

At this stage it is useful to establish a small team of staff who will drive the literacy project forward.

First steps
Year 1, September and October

Many schools carry out an audit, possibly issuing questionnaires to teachers to gauge opinion of the issues linked with literacy. These can return comments that are not particularly useful; it will not help generate momentum to discover that some staff are lukewarm about literacy or cross-curricular collaboration.

It is more fruitful to involve a small group of students straight away, by inviting them to become *literacy tutors*, generating literacy resources and teaching other students. For more detail of how this might be done see strategy 2, 'How to run a literacy assembly' (see page 25) and strategy 39, 'Involving students as leaders of literacy and learning in subjects other than English' (see page 155).

Observing lessons from a literacy point of view, by conducting a *literacy learning walk*, (see strategy 49, page 201), will begin the process of envisaging the potential of a cross-curricular strategy. In conducting our learning walks we devised a four-point scale similar to that used by Ofsted; the Ofsted framework in place from January 2012 makes explicit reference to the development of cross-curricular skills, but we devised this scheme to focus specifically on literacy. We chose to visit science lessons, and found striking examples of missed opportunities, for example in a Year 7 lesson, students were researching animals and writing leaflets but were not giving any thought of how leaflets are written or how best to read for information. Examples like this will be very useful when outlining the literacy strategy to colleagues.

If you do not already do so, you might wish to *assess incoming students for spelling or reading age*: this data will enable you to target support, and may be useful for evaluating progress later on. (Strategies 25, 26 and 27 – pages 100 to 113 – give more detail on how you might approach spelling.)

Raising awareness with staff
Year 1, November and December

It is important to make use of existing school activities and structures. We chose to use a pre-existing event, the annual Year 7 book review that takes place in November. Part of an extensive transfer programme, students in Year 7 bring in all their books which are set out in the school library, in tutor groups. Traditionally, Year 7 tutors meet Year 6 teachers to discuss the progress of the pupils they have taught.

We took advantage of this event to add a *work scrutiny* (strategy 6 on page 35), which you might like to introduce as a regular event. All heads of subject and pastoral leaders were invited to review a selection of books: each member of staff was asked to look at a minimum of three students' work, of high, middle and low ability on entry, using Cognitive Ability Tests (CATs) or SATs results. After the work scrutiny we discussed the findings with colleagues. It is also possible to share examples of writing pupils are capable of in primary schools, to raise the question – can we show progress from Key Stage 2?

A meeting like this provides an opportunity to raise the issues about transition, and to compare the experience of students in primary schools with that in many secondary schools. For students who are insecure writers – for example, those who are not confident using paragraphs or complex sentences – how much practice and support at writing are they receiving across the curriculum? How consistently is writing supported across the curriculum?

This discussion should allow many key ideas to be raised, and key action points decided: our first work scrutiny revealed that, after ten weeks in school, students had done almost no extended writing, which we simply defined as writing more than one sentence!

The first training session for staff can share the findings of the work scrutiny and showcase the work of the literacy tutors. This is an opportunity to set out the goals for the literacy strategy; one easy-to-set goal is that the annual Year 7 work scrutiny shows progress in written work. Staff may want to carry out other work scrutinies, for example, with different year groups. You may also wish to look at work completed in primary schools – see strategy 5 (page 33).

Using assemblies to raise student awareness
Year 1, November and December

Using strategy 2, 'How to run a literary assembly' (see page 25), to raise the profile of literacy is a way of ensuring that staff and students hear the same message. This is an opportunity to invite students to sign up for membership of the *literacy steering group* (see strategy 8, page 41). This group can start to meet, perhaps once per term.

Staff training, literacy and examinations
Year 1, January

At a staff training meeting, working with staff groups of between 20 and 30, hold a discussion of *the role of literacy in exam papers* (see strategy 7, page 38). This can lead to a mapping exercise, to be completed by the end of the summer term, and the idea of a *Litweb* (see strategy 17, page 73) can be launched. This resource should be accessible to students and parents at home and school, located on the school website or a virtual learning environment.

Using assemblies to launch the idea of literacy leaders and the Litweb
Year 1, February and March

In the second series of assemblies, outline in some detail the ways in which students can be involved, as *literacy leaders* (see strategy 43, page 171) and contributors to the Litweb.

Learning walks and work scrutinies for Year 8 groups and above
Year 1, April and May

At this stage it is helpful to gather more information about the teaching of literacy across the school. Ideally, key staff and one or two subject or pastoral leaders, should be involved in observing lessons and carrying out work scrutinies. If you can find examples of good practice these can be shared with colleagues.

Working with primary schools
Year 1, May onwards

Primary liaison is a key feature of our programme. In order to address the decline in the quality of written work that can occur when pupils transfer from primary to secondary schools we asked each primary school to provide a benchmark piece of writing, to be collected before the end of the summer term (see strategy 5, page 33). If you plan to hold the work scrutiny of Year 7 books in November, primary colleagues can be invited at this point.

Mapping opportunities for reading, writing, speaking and listening
Year 1, June and July

As part of the normal planning cycle it is possible to map out the activities that support literacy across the curriculum and produce an *entitlement grid* (see strategy 1, page 23). This is also an opportunity to do further work on the Litweb.

Evaluating progress
Year 1, July

Before the end of the year you can retest students for spelling and reading age using tests such as the Neale, Schonnell, NFER Group Reading Tests or the Salford Sentence Test. This data can be used alongside teacher assessments to evaluate progress, but also to identify students who need further support.

You may also like to sample books or interview students to gather more information about the progress of cross-curricular literacy.

Engaging parents and building consistency
Year 2, September and October

At the start of the year copies of the *benchmark* pieces of work (see strategy 5, page 33) can be stuck in each exercise book, alongside other departmental information about expectations for the completion of written work.

We took advantage of the thorough programme of support at the point of transition that already exists at our school to engage parents in the literacy village. At an evening for parents explain ways in which they can support the development of reading and writing. You can outline the concept of the benchmark pieces of work, and encourage parents to read and monitor the quality of homework. You can invite parents to volunteer as literacy tutors. (See strategies 45 to 49, pages 186 to 203.)

Planning future developments with the literacy steering group
Year 2, October

The students on the steering group will now be familiar with the whole school literacy drive and will be in a position to make informed comments about opportunities to make further progress. This is a good point to look at the *whole-school marking policy* (see strategies 26 and 27, pages 103 to 113). Does it support literacy? Is it working in practice?

Students may come up with other suggestions: for example activities to support *reading for pleasure* (strategy 35, page 141), literacy awards or a literacy newsletter.

Reviewing progress: the Year 7 work scrutiny
Year 2, November

Carrying out the work scrutiny in the same way that you did it in the first year of the literacy programme provides an opportunity to gauge progress. For example, you might ask colleagues to focus on the following questions:

- Are the benchmark pieces stuck into each book?
- Is there evidence of progression from Year 6 – or at least of sustaining the quality of writing?
- Is there evidence of a development in the quality of written work compared to last year?

Revising the whole school marking policy
Year 2, December

It is likely that students and the work scrutiny will have revealed inconsistency in the application of the school marking policy. This feedback can be the starting point for updating the policy. The aim should be to ensure that, every time a student writes, they are encouraged to write accurately and effectively; spellings should be addressed, using a common approach; most importantly, students should be doing something in response to the teachers' marking.

Consolidating improvements
Year 2, January and February

By now there should be a wide range of activities taking place in school, but take-up will vary from one team to another. Using a range of monitoring activities such as those outlined above (work scrutinies, interviews with students and lesson observations) allows you to evaluate progress and provides evidence for celebrating success, with students in assemblies and with staff in training sessions.

You may have detailed progress data available (for example, from RaiseOnline). Putting this together with any data you have collected – for example, information from CATs testing or reading and spelling data – might allow you to see patterns. Do students with below average skills in literacy underperform, not only in the traditionally word-based subjects but also, for example, in maths?

Improving the quality of oral work across the curriculum
Year 2, March

The focus of many of the activities so far has been on written work. Using criteria from the GCSE English syllabus used by your school and national curriculum descriptors for oral work, it is possible to offer staff and students guidance on developing discussion work. Carrying out a simple moderation of levels or grades, using an exam board video or one prepared in school, will give staff more confidence in promoting higher attainment in speaking and listening. Useful resources can be collected on the Litweb.

Exam preparation: command words and conventions for writing
Year 2, April and May

When preparing students for exams, most staff focus on the questions that are set and the precise meaning of instructions on exam papers. Sharing information, producing a glossary or guide to command words and conventions of writing for exam courses, which points out the precise meaning of similar terms in different contexts is a task the literacy steering group can take on.

School development plan and a whole-school literacy policy
Year 2, June and July

By now a wide variety of literacy activities will be in place across the curriculum. Using a variety of evaluative tools the school can decide on future priorities and integrate these into the school development plan. This is a good point at which to draw together the various policies and documents produced into one *whole school literacy policy* (see strategy 53, page 221).

It is important that monitoring and evaluation activities ensure a relentless focus on striving for high standards. Examples of how this may be done are included in Part 4 'Evaluating impact'.

PART 2

Putting your Literacy Programme into Practice

1 The Beginning stage

This first section includes strategies for getting your programme started. Pick and choose those strategies that help you start. Remember: keep focused, don't try and do everything; be patient.

Strategy 1 Ensure consistency of writing across the curriculum

Literacy Outcomes

- Students have the opportunity to produce writing in a wide variety of genres.
- Staff across different subjects work together to ensure consistent messages and high-quality written work.

Getting started

At primary school, students are used to producing different kinds of writing in science, humanities or project work and there will be a consistency of message. In the early years of secondary school, however, students produce far less writing than one might expect and there is far less consistency of expectations transcending the different subjects. One of the first steps towards developing a consistent writing approach across the curriculum, is to map out the opportunities students have to write in different genres.

Putting it into practice

At a staff meeting or training session, introduce the aim: to produce a map of the type of writing students are asked to produce across the curriculum. You might like to start with Year 7 or the first Year group you have in the school. Explain that the aim is to share information and ensure consistency of advice given to students. This will help in the sharing of resources and expectations.

Before the session, draw up a simple questionnaire asking the following questions:

- What type of writing do you ask students to produce? Letters, reports, diaries?
- How do you explain the conventions of the genre?
- How do you support students who find writing difficult? How do you extend more able students?

- Where can students find exemplars of good work?

Invite teachers to complete the questionnaire and compile a spreadsheet of your findings (there is an example online). You now have your entitlement grid, which you can analyse for any obvious patterns or gaps: which genres are absent? Which could be introduced more effectively?

Taking it further

- Meet with colleagues and discuss your findings. Discuss exactly what you mean by certain genres, and the conventions you teach. You may start to find some contradictions as well as some common ground.

- Combine the meeting and discussion of the entitlement grid with an element of work scrutiny: how can you improve the quality of written work? This discussion may lead to other activities discussed elsewhere, for example, the sharing of good practice via the Litweb.

What the staff say

As you might expect, we have always encouraged a variety of written work, right from Year 7. We use letter writing, diaries and newspapers, as well as traditional essays. We're quite good at discussing as a team what we are looking for in terms of our own subject specific skills – and we have even included a mark for literacy – but what we haven't done until now is think about how we teach the writing skills. I think we assume that that happens somewhere else. This exercise is a good first step for us – and has meant we have started to think more carefully about how to improve the quality of the writing we get students to do.

Head of history

Links to other strategies

- Strategy 5 'How to raise expectations of writing by looking at work completed in primary schools' on page 33.
- Strategy 6 'How to set up a work scrutiny for cross-curricular literacy' on page 35.

Strategy 2 How to run a literacy assembly

Literacy Outcomes

- Staff are trained in key literacy skills.
- Students receive a consistent message about the whole school literacy focus.
- The whole school sees the importance of literacy in all subjects.

Getting started

Ask your assembly coordinator for a series of about six assemblies across the year. These can be with a particular year group or the whole school. Whoever manages your school's assembly programme will be delighted that you are offering your services. All the better if you've got senior management backing and literacy is a whole-school priority. But more of that later.

Putting it into practice

Let's suppose you have Year 7 in front of you and 15 minutes to deliver your messages. You've planned out your six assemblies. They might be titled as follows:

- Why literacy launches space ships
- How punctuation can change your world
- Paragraphs and how to give them superpowers
- The secret of the comma
- Why colons make you cool
- The semi-colon and the meaning of life.

Your focus might be, as in this example, internal sentence construction and extended writing. But whatever it is, making a big truthful claim about why the skill you're teaching is important. Try to get the students involved in delivering the assembly with you. Reciprocal teaching is more likely to help retention. When students speak with you, other students and even staff pay a different kind of attention. Clearly you'll need to rehearse them, but the pay-off is significant. Ideas and advice for running literacy assemblies include:

- *Use an image.* In 'Why literacy launches space ships,' you could have a NASA image of the far side of Jupiter. They are readily available via NASA's website. Simply display the image and then ask, 'Where do you think this is?' Someone will always have a go at answering and you should praise this bravery. Then ask, 'What launched the spaceship Voyager 9, which travelled 93 billion miles into space to take the picture and transmit it back to earth?' The students will have all kinds of answers from 'petrol' to 'magic'. Then you reveal that it was, in fact, the semi-colon. Students will find this somewhat dubious. So your next slide is an extract from the Voyager's propulsion manual. It's a dazzling mixture of formulae, equations and, critically, explanation rhetoric. And if you zoom in to this instruction manual, you'll see it is crammed with internal punctuation, connectives and paragraphing. So you tell them, for example, 'Today, in your science lesson, you may be able to write yourself into the stars. Without these skills, the spaceship could not have been built, launched or flown.'

- *Use questions.* The more you can involve the students in guessing and spotting the punctuation, the better.

- *Use music.* If your assembly has a dramatic atmosphere, this is going to help retention.

- *Use a cliffhanger: another image.* This time show a plant, or a fast car, or a wad of bank notes. Ask how they were produced. Tell them it was all thanks to paragraphing and you'll prove it to them next time. Then show an extract from a gardening manual, a car manufacture process, a 'get rich quick' guide: you need them to see that punctuation will always be necessary.

- *Address the staff at the same time as the students.* One of the keys to the success of this approach is that you are also helping the staff who may lack confidence with the more abstruse forms of punctuation. Quite often adults don't like to admit they have skill gaps in literacy and an assembly like this allows them, safely, to find out what you want them to teach.

Taking it further

- Your assembly can be a whole-staff briefing led by students.
- Train a few students to show the staff what works: modelled writing, for instance.

- Ask students to lead a piece of writing on what makes an effective lesson, for example. It is always surprising how brave some students will be, and the effect can be more powerful than if staff lead staff.
- Turn these assemblies into podcasts, blogs or vlogs posted on your school's Virtual Learning Environment (VLE) or website. This is especially interesting, for example, when a student allows their voice to be overlaid on an image of a favourite book, or piece of writing, and then played to an assembly or class, via the VLE.

What the students say

I found this a really useful way to think about how language can influence things. I hadn't made a link between spacecraft and writing and I'm really into space things. It was brilliant when I could show the staff the blog I'd made. It was about Phillip Pullman's book, *Northern Lights*. I was asked to show my PowerPoint in one of the weekly staff meetings. It was strange having a hundred teachers looking at me and listening to me. But that just made me feel more brave. I was so pleased to show the PowerPoint I'd made.

I'm really glad to be able to use Prezi. Now I use it all the time: some teachers don't know what it is. But it helps us focus on types of writing that we think are important, like the use of commas, colons and semi-colons.

Classes like zooming in and out of types of writing. I really liked taking the year group on a sort of journey through types of writing and showing them what I think is important.

Curtis, aged 14

What the staff say

I was sceptical at first, as with anything that has the aura of 'new initiative'. But it felt comfortable to hear how literacy works when we were shown strategies and even reminded what key language terms meant. I had forgotten how the semi-colon worked. I felt safe being reminded of its function in an assembly format. It was especially helpful to see a piece of writing from technology that used a variety of punctuation.

In some assemblies, we heard students explaining why internal punctuation helped. I couldn't believe the attention the students' peers gave this exposition.

Anne, technology teacher

Strategy 3 Choosing the literacy focus for your school

Literacy Outcomes

- Staff have a clear idea of the focus and direction for future literacy work.
- Staff have the opportunity to discuss issues of literacy that are important to them.

Getting started

At some stage you will want to decide on the focus for your literacy activities for the first year of the project. This type of discussion and decision making may follow some activities undertaken to raise awareness and gather information. Alternatively, you may have a clear idea of areas of relative strength and weakness as result of an analysis of exam results or response to an inspection visit.

If you have not done so already, in preparation for a meeting of your steering group, carry out one or more of the following activities: work scrutinies, lesson observations, analysis of exam results or interviews with students.

While you might not have a clear idea of the detail of strengths and weaknesses in your school, you probably have general impressions which you can test out.

Putting it into practice

Call a steering group meeting and invite key members of staff: this is likely to include heads of key subject areas including English, humanities, and science. At this meeting, share the findings of your initial research. As your starting point, take some of the key pieces of information you have to hand, for example, performance in GCSE exams in written subjects. You may then want to set a target, for example, raising attainment in English or raising attainment in humanities subjects generally. If you can make specific targets, this will help monitoring later on.

Given that many different activities impact on achievement in literacy, you may want to discuss a range of possibilities before settling on your final focus, for example:

- Oracy, including discussion work and presentations.
- Reading, including reading for pleasure, particularly fiction and factual reading, including research.
- Writing.
- You may want to focus on a particular key stage.
- You may decide to launch a number of different initiatives at the same time, knowing that one will support another.

By the end of the meeting, agree on three fairly specific areas in which you will work. Use different sections in this book to identify key strategies and decide who will take responsibility for which activity.

Taking it further

- If you already have a fairly strong idea of the key areas you wish to work on, you might like to combine this meeting with a work scrutiny, or you may wish to involve students or your literacy steering group in the discussion.
- Depending on the readiness of colleagues in your school, you may wish to carry out a series of fairly detailed observations, perhaps using the evaluation strategies in 'Evaluating impact' (see page 196 onwards).

What the staff say

I remember hearing the phrase 'Every teacher is a teacher of English' on my PGCE – and I know we have done some work on language across the curriculum, but as an A-level teacher I get increasingly frustrated by the poor quality of written work many produce. Anything we can do to improve it can only be for the good.

Geography teacher

Links to other strategies

- Strategy 49 'How to evaluate the quality of literacy teaching: lesson observations and learning walks' on page 201.

Strategy 4 How to design a Literacy Box

Literacy Outcomes

- All classrooms will have a Literacy Box.
- Students and staff will feel more confident about the use of literacy terms in their various subject domains.
- Students will experience a sense of leadership within the lesson.

Getting started

Providing staff with a Literacy Box shows them they can improve literacy in their lesson, whatever their subject, with little time input from themselves. Try to assure staff that using the Literacy Box will

- be low cost
- be low technology
- not impede content delivery
- develop student leadership
- require little or no pre-lesson preparation.

Obviously, the more that staff commit, the more they will get out of it. But, by placing the Literacy Box and other strategies into the hands of their students, they will make significant gains.

Putting it into practice

Get some large plastic boxes. Create a set of laminated resources for students to display during the lesson and use as part of modelled writing. Then, at a staff meeting tell staff they all have a gift to take away – the Literacy Box or 'Litbox'. Explain to them this is a box containing easy-to-use resources demonstrating key language terms.

You will find in the online resources a Litbox to get you started. It contains a variety of resources ready for your adaptation, for example: groups of connectives;

examples of styles of writing; command words, definitions and examples used by examination boards

Tell the staff that this is an offer rather than a requirement, suggesting that they might even have fun with the resource. Show and tell them, briefly how to use it; the most effective way is for the teacher to give the Literacy Box to a student and have them post the key language terms around the room. This means the teacher can get on with subject-specific content delivery. The student chooses whatever they think might be important.

We found it helpful to have as few items as possible in the box; connectives work well because they are generally important in most cross-curricular writing genres. Have the connectives colour grouped by type. So, use different colours for connectives of difference, connectives of similarity, connectives for describing effects and connectives of flair. Reassure staff that the contents of the Literacy box will encourage student curiosity; it is the ethos that questioning and wondering enhances high-quality learning.

Taking it further

- At the introductory session have students explain to the staff how students can help; they can demonstrate the simplicity of posting the key language terms so that the class can see them.

- Emphasising the invitational nature of this strategy encourages its acceptance. The Literacy Box is a gift. Staff can use it where they think fit.

- Combining the resource introduction with training a group of students to be literacy leaders further increases the likelihood of acceptance.

What the students say

I did feel a bit nervous standing in front of the staff, but they were on my side, and when I showed them how easy it is to Blu-Tack the words and phrases round the room, they were won over. And when I've done this in lessons, everyone looks at what I'm doing and pays attention to the words. They don't know what they all mean. But we try them out and see which fits best.

James, aged 14

Strategy 5 How to raise expectations of writing by looking at work completed in primary schools

Literacy Outcomes

- Staff have a better idea of what Year 6 students can do.
- Staff have a benchmark – a standard of work to expect across the curriculum.

Getting started

The Key Stage 2 staff in your partner schools are a tremendous resource. Students may well be producing written work of far greater complexity across the curriculum than you might expect in Key Stage 2. Any activities you can do that allow Key Stage 3 teachers to realise this are of great benefit in your drive to raise standards.

Visit Year 6 lessons and ask the teachers to collect a number of examples of writing for you to copy and share with colleagues.

Putting it into practice

At a staff meeting, possibly a middle leaders' staff meeting, share examples of written work from Key Stage 2. Aim to include work that will be surprising because of its depth, detail and sophistication. Even if only a few of your students produce this kind of work it shows what you need to build on in Key Stage 3 and the targets you can aim for. You might give a range of work, with some examples of levelled work as benchmarks, and get staff to level the writing. You can usually engineer it so that staff are surprised by the quality of the Key Stage 2 work. You may well be able to track a decline in the quality of writing in Key Stage 3 and into Key Stage 4 by certain students – for example, middle-ability boys – as they stop thinking about the quality of their writing across the curriculum.

Taking it further

- Use the bridging units and transfer books that students start in Key Stage 2 and bring with them, to ensure you have a benchmark, a standard you will build on. Often these will be seen only by English teachers.

- Alternatively, it is far more effective to ask primary colleagues to get all students to produce one piece of writing that can serve as a benchmark. Ask each primary teacher to provide a piece of writing on one side of A4 that represents good quality writing from each student, produced in half an hour. This should not be redrafted. Ensure the work shows the name of the student clearly on the page. When you have collected these pieces, photocopy them (possibly on A5 stickers): there needs to be enough copies for each student to stick a copy of the work into each of their exercise books or folders. During tutor time in Year 7 make sure a copy is stuck into every book. This resource provides an easy way of assessing the quality of writing produced in Year 7, which is ideal for monitoring progress.

What the staff say

As a parent of two primary-age children I am well aware of the types of writing they do, really from Key Stage 1 onwards, and certainly by the end of Key Stage 2 – but I don't think all my colleagues are. I think for some of us it comes as a bit of a shock to see what they can do. Sometimes, because we are always in a bit of a hurry, we tend to rush things and then assume that the brief pieces of scruffy work students do for us are the limit of their ability.

Teacher of design technology

Links to other strategies

- Strategy 6 'How to set up a work scrutiny for cross-curricular literacy' on page 35.

Strategy 6 How to set up a work scrutiny for cross-curricular literacy

Literacy Outcomes

- Staff awareness of literacy is raised.
- Staff expectations of what students are capable of is raised.
- Opportunities to discuss literacy in a cross-curricular group are created.

Getting started

Choose a focus: restricting your sample to one Year group makes the process simpler and discussions can be more specific. Year 7 works very well, because you can raise all sorts of issues relating to transfer.

Collect a sample of books across all subjects. Make sure they are representative of all abilities. Having too many books is better than too few; staff will wonder whether the sample is representative, so having more books on hand to check is useful. One simple way to do the scrutiny is to ask the first five students on the register from each tutor group to bring all of their books to a central room; we have tended to use our library.

Each member of staff taking part will need the following:

- A list of students with Key Stage 2 data, and whatever else you have – for example CATs information.
- Examples of written work at level 4 and level 5.
- A sheet, or set of sheets, on which to record their findings.

You might want to involve all your middle leaders, including those with curriculum and pastoral responsibility, and anyone else who is interested.

Putting it into practice

Invite your selection of school leaders and opinion formers to the meeting, which will probably take one hour. Arrange for your sample of students to bring their books. Arrange them in piles for each child. When staff arrive give them a sheet showing the key data for the students – Key Stage 2 data, or anything that shows prior ability. You may put names of staff against a number of students to ensure spread. As a minimum, ask staff to look at the books of three students, of above average, middle, and below average ability. Ask staff to complete notes in answer to a number of the following questions. You may like to choose two or three to focus on:

- Are standards in literacy high enough?
- Are students at all levels producing writing at level 4 or level 5? (Your examples of written work at these levels may help make a judgment.)
- Are students producing written work that shows they have made progress in literacy since Key Stage 2?
- Which subjects are encouraging students to produce the best writing? How?
- How many examples of extended writing can you find?
- Are high expectations of accuracy being reinforced?
- Does assessment by staff and students support literacy?
- Are staff explicitly teaching the literacy skills required in their subject?

After a given time – probably 30 or 40 minutes – gather staff together to discuss findings. You might want to use a good piece of writing produced in Key Stage 1 or 2 as an example. Key Stage 3 and 4 teachers, even those used to working in writing-based subjects, are often surprised to discover what children can do. You may find some books where literacy is excellent: use the teachers who have produced these books to inspire and help you lead others. You may learn that staff have found very few examples of extended writing. If this is so, what is the reason?

Staff may well say they do not have the time to focus on writing: at this point it may be useful to remind them of the centrality of written work to many forms of assessment in secondary schools. Many staff may also lack confidence in their literacy skills and will say that they would do more, if only they felt more confident: at this point you can share your ideas for staff training and further support.

By the end of a session like this you will have raised interest, and possibly created some feelings of disappointment or discontent: this is a vital step towards generating energy to produce change.

Taking it further

- Some staff may argue that evidence of writing will be clearer later in the year, or in the year above: you might like to repeat this exercise with a different group of students.
- You may be able to involve your primary colleagues who will be interested to see how the students they taught are progressing.
- Repeat the process next year to see how much progress you are making.
- Templates for questionnaires and a PowerPoint to use with staff at the meeting are available online.

What the staff say

To be honest I was a bit shocked by what we found when we did this. I think many of us assumed that everyone else was doing something, and that our turn would be next. There are lots of things we are keen to do in Year 7, but we musn't forget some of these basic things. All students need to practise their core skills, otherwise they are bound to forget them.

PE teacher

I don't think we have enough opportunities to discuss students' work. You always learn something when you do. This is such a good opportuntiy to do just that.

Psychology and sociology teacher

Links to other strategies

- Strategy 5 'How to raise expectations of writing by looking at work completed in primary schools' on page 33 which shows how a work scrutiny can fit into a year's programme of transfer activities.

Strategy 7 How to share an understanding of the literacy element of different exam papers

Literacy Outcomes

- Staff working in different subjects see links with other subjects.
- Staff realise the significance of literacy for students sitting exams.
- Staff begin to see the potential for links and collaboration.

Getting started

Invite colleagues to a meeting to share ideas about improving exam performance by concentrating on the reading demands of examinations. Prepare in advance by collecting in examples of as many exam papers as possible – at least ten, at various levels including GCSE. Look for examples with texts, either pre-release or to be read in the examination room.

Putting it into practice

Invite colleagues to work in pairs and rank the exam papers in terms of reading difficulty. After ten minutes, share the outcomes. Raise some of the following questions – there are additional points included which you might like to use for guidance.

Which paper had the highest reading demands?

- It is not always the obvious papers, for example, English or history, that are the most difficult.
- Maths pre-release papers for statistics can contain long passages of abstract text.
- Science pre-release material can look very similar to English reading exam papers.
- Sports studies or GCSE papers can contain complex vocabulary, Latinate and medical terms, sometimes presented without context.

If students have this complex range of reading challenges, how do we develop the skills they need?

- How does each subject team teach students how to read an exam paper?

- Do teachers explicitly analyse the features of the text? So, for example, does the science teacher show the structure of the piece of writing – how topic sentences are used, how an introduction sets out the key arguments and so on?

- Do teachers help students develop reading skills, by teaching them how to tackle a written text, or do they encourage students to develop bad habits, answering questions without reading a text properly?

- Do teachers use texts with students that are too difficult and thus do not develop skills in tackling them, for example, by reading the text to the students?

Do staff work together effectively?

- Are there opportunities to develop strategies that can be shared across the school, for example, posters, reminders, revision resources that teach shared-reading strategies?

- Do English teachers work in science lessons modelling how to analyse a text?

Are there shared resources you can develop?

- This might include a list of examination keywords, often command words, what they mean and imply. These could be put into a table, for example: 'Evaluate: In geography this means…In English we are expected to…'

At the end of the meeting agree three simple strategies that the school can adopt.

Taking it further

- If you have time to prepare more fully, you can be more specific about the literacy challenges of exam papers.

- Film some of your students reading exam papers aloud to indicate the difficulties they may have in decoding them.

- Film a discussion you have had with students about the different ways teachers approach reading exam papers.
- Use a simple piece of software to calculate the reading age of some of the exam papers; compare this with the reading ages of some of your students.

What the staff say

As a PE teacher it was good to hear – for once – that staff were aware that we do have some difficult literacy issues to tackle. A lot of staff think back to their own schooling, and I guess not many will have done exams in our subject

Head of PE

We do quite a bit of work on command words, but we still have students saying that they don't understand certain words, or that they mean different things in different subjects. Sometimes we have to be clear with them – we know that the word has a slightly different meaning in this context, but they have to be flexible and learn the differences. We have to make clear that, for the purposes of exam, when it says 'describe' and 'explain' they get the marks for explaining only if they link it to the description they have given. The more we can make this kind of thing explicit to students the better. It helps if we can make clear, accurate references to what they have done in other subjects – not just guessing!

Head of science

Links to other strategies

- Strategy 1 'Crossing the divide: ensuring that all students have an entitlement' on page 23.
- Strategy 8 'How to share an understanding of the literacy element of different exam papers' on page 41.

Strategy 8 How to set up a literacy steering group

Literacy Outcomes

- Students will be actively engaged in the process of developing literacy.
- You will have easy access to a source of ideas and feedback, a ready-made focus group.
- Students can help do some of the work in sharing ideas and good practice.

Getting started

Use literacy assemblies to start the process of developing awareness and stimulating interest. Invite students and staff to become part of the 'literacy village'. Ask for student volunteers to join a steering group: aim for a manageable number, maybe 16 or so, and invite them to a meeting.

Alternatively, ask all your staff to invite at least two students from each of the classes they teach to become literacy leaders. Invite all these students to two or three literacy assemblies. At such events, ask which students are prepared to take a lead in improvement of literacy in the school. There are always a number of students that are curious enough to want to know what this is about; that's what you want. Invite them to another meeting: this can be during tutor, PHSE, or English time. All three subject areas can support what you are doing: encouraging innovation, literacy and team building.

When you meet, invite these students to become part of a formal literacy steering group. If they accept, there are the following rewards:

- Improving the school's learning of literacy.
- Helping to invent and plan whole school literacy strategies, such as the whole-school marking policy.
- Getting to talk and even teach the entire staff.
- UCAS personal statement benefits.

- A place on the school's VLE and website to promote literacy in all its forms, especially writing and reading.
- Letters of praise home and to tutors.

Putting it into practice

Have a very clear, practical focus for the literacy steering group. This means that students, and any staff involved, can see an obvious impact from their work. We have found focusing on marking for literacy and reading for pleasure to be very rewarding activities. You may wish to give your literacy steering group the challenge of promoting reading for pleasure in a specific Year group or Key Stage: for further detail, see the strategy 35 'How to support reading for pleasure across the curriculum' on page 141.

Because students are the primary consumers of our marking they have very interesting comments to make on the process. Ask students to bring along examples of marked work – preferably including examples where they feel the marking has really helped, and where it is less successful. When we carried out this exercise we also invited students to read our marking policy. When asked, 'When your work is marked, what helps you make progress?' students said:

- 'When my work is marked I make progress if the teacher speaks to me about it and how I can improve.'
- 'When teachers make you read the comments.'
- 'It helps when teachers put the correct spelling next to the mistake.'
- 'Evaluation of work in a small sentence. Correct spelling to be put in when a mistake is made.'
- 'Constructive criticisms, targets, tips to improve work.'
- 'Explanation: the teacher must provide reasoning to give the student a better understanding of the error and why.'
- 'Discussion time with teacher one to one, looking through work, talking about improvements.'

When asked, 'When your work is marked, what is less successful?' students said:

- 'When the teachers just write "sp" or "incomplete sentence" then it doesn't really mean much because you don't know what to improve on.'

- 'When my work is marked it says that I have made a spelling mistake however it does not say how to put it right.'
- 'Always focusing on the bad.'
- 'When the teacher messes up a piece of neat work with a red pen.'
- 'Highlighting errors with no follow-up, not showing correct spelling.'
- 'Work being given back with no time to look through, not being able to read teacher's handwriting.'

Students invariably tell it like it is. When asked, 'What do you think of our current marking policy?' they said:

- 'Quite good if you're amazing at knowing grammar and not making mistakes.'
- 'It's not very good because it doesn't show you how to improve.'

Be prepared to listen and take on board your students' comments. After hearing our students' comments on our spelling and marking policy we set about redrafting it.

Taking it further

Meet your steering group regularly; invite them to help you plan and monitor your literacy activities. They may well provide a source of literacy leaders for any activities you carry out: our literacy steering group helped plan the conference on literacy and leadership we ran at school.

Consider analysing what the data about the school tells you about where you need to go. In our experience, exposing students to selected performance data can have a positive effect; after all, they see it in the national and local media. Analysis at the small-group level of what lies behind the blunt published headlines is an important and revealing journey. It also seems to appeal to a competitive nature many students use to drive their achievement. This can be used to help the achievement of others, mainly out of a loyalty to the school but students also report they find it rewarding to help others. All you need to do is direct them to the pages that illustrate the overall progress being made by students in English. In the UK's 'RAISE documents', for example, students will easily pick up that anything over 1000 is positive. Most students want their school to improve. Giving them access to some nationally recognised data is letting them into the 'secret garden' of performance indicators.

Discuss with students what you find in your work trawl monitoring. This has positive benefits because students are often surprised by how good much of the writing is. Make sure to keep work anonymous, of course. Your steering group will inevitably be cross-ability and they can identify with students of different ages and strengths.

Plan a year's calendar of literacy events, for example:

- Launch the classroom literacy leader programme.
- Use three assemblies to remind students the components of your literacy focus (for example, connectives, internal punctuation and paragraphs).
- Plan an annual literacy conference. This is a day-long event to which you invite any local school to bring along a couple of staff and up to six students. Activities could include sharing what you are doing, including successes and barriers; splitting into cross-school groups to co-develop literacy materials to take away; discussing with the staff how to engage and sustain the literacy project through students' co-leadership.
- Invite a writer or actor to the school and ask him or her to talk with the students about the fears and obstacles they had to overcome. These will be the same in most cases as those faced by students.

What the students say

I think the steering group is very important. I think it helps teachers, because in a way we know about some things that they don't. We ought to be involved in things like the marking and spelling policy because we are the ones who need to learn from it.

Declan, Year 10

Links to other strategies

- Strategy 27 'How to produce a spelling and marking policy' on page 109.
- Strategy 31 'How to support reading for pleasure across the curriculum' on page 129.

2 The Embedding Stage

This section includes strategies to help build enthusiasm for your literacy programme and the activities are designed to help you keep the school focused on your literacy project. Adopt and adapt those with which you think your school can cope with.

Strategy 9 How to teach punctuation to the science department

Literacy Outcomes

- Colleagues feel a little more confident with both basic and more elaborate punctuation.
- Colleagues get a chance to ask questions about punctuation.
- Colleagues share thoughts on effective means of making content memorable.

Getting started

Understandably, many staff don't want to admit what they don't know about literacy. So, start with a game and try to take the pressure off the non-specialist staff as much as possible. We want colleagues to have fun and enjoy literacy games and so that they will try them with their students.

Stress to the staff that they can take part in the game if they wish. There will always be at least half the department who will give it a go. You are in the business of creating allies. If you have even a quarter of the science team committed to the whole school literacy project, this constitutes a critical mass. The spread of enthusiasm and knowledge is necessarily slow. We found that it took 24 months for the roots of the literacy project to grow. If you think that a single INSET day will secure commitment, you are unlikely to be successful. Whole-school change happens over a longer period of time. Tell staff what to do and you will encounter resistance. Have staff and students report success, infiltrate subject and Year teams in an unobtrusive, open, friendly manner and you are more likely to gain the allegiance you need.

Putting it into practice

Say to staff: 'Everyone think of a punctuation mark. Now tell the person next to you what that is.' Next say: 'Tell the person next to you what job that punctuation mark does. For example, if you thought of a full stop, tell them that it is used to end sentences.'

Role-play an element of punctuation and invite the science team to hot seat you. Choose something relatively obscure, for example: the ellipsis or semi-colon. This is an easy, non-threatening strategy where all that your colleagues have to do is ask whatever they like about purpose, usage, value of the punctuation mark you have elected to be. Allow questions of any sort, depending on how brave you're feeling. In this role-play scenario, staff might feel more comfortable to ask questions they might otherwise not have done. If you think the staff are likely to be reticent, have sample questions pre-printed as a 'lucky dip'. Questions could include:

- 'What do you do?'
- 'Why do you matter?'
- What else would do instead?'
- 'What's your opposite?'
- 'Give me an example of you in action.'

Be as adventurous as you can. By encouraging slightly more imaginative questions, it's more likely your colleagues will remember the content and talk about it afterwards. For example, personify the punctuation mark by encouraging questions such as:

- 'Who is your best friend?'
- 'What do you do if no one uses you?'
- 'How important do you feel?'
- 'What's your chemical make up?'
- 'What movies do you like?'
- 'What's your favourite food?'

The more bizarre the better. It is crucial to establish a sense of play. The department meeting where you introduce this needs to be relaxed and open to experiment.

Taking it further

Say to staff, 'Let's have a go at the Punctuation Party. When I say let the party begin, you get up and introduce yourself to your colleagues saying, 'Hi, I'm a full stop.' Then make it more adventurous: 'OK, now meet at least three people and tell them what you are and what you do.' Finally: 'Meet any two people and act in the manner of the punctuation mark's personality.' You'll find a range of reactions, including full stops that strut, commas that act deferentially, semi-colons that are quietly proud. The point is to play.

Say to your colleagues that this game can be played as a starter or plenary whenever they wish. Even if students get definitions or purposes wrong, they can correct them.

What the staff say

Yes we thought this was silly at first. But then we just gave it a go and more people than we expected took part. It encouraged talk and questions about language. Not everyone knew what the punctuation marks were. It gave us a safe environment to ask questions we dared not ask, like, 'What does an ellipsis do?'

Jennifer, science teacher

Strategy 10 How learning in modern foreign languages can be a key vehicle for improving literacy

Literacy Outcome

- Students apply the language terms used in modern foreign languages across the curriculum.

Getting started

Colleagues in the modern foreign languages (MFL) team say to us that they value teachers across the school knowing basic language terms. This is very helpful in the whole school literacy project. Teachers of MFL want their students to understand grammatical knowledge such as the use of connectives and the accurate use of internal punctuation (commas, colons and sub-clauses).

So, we ask them what connectives most improve their students' writing. This is school dependent, but we find that connectives of comparison and evaluation are often the most useful.

Ask MFL colleagues to nominate literacy leaders. We find that students will enjoy taking leadership roles, especially if they know it isn't going to be forever; we found the length of one term works well. They can work in groups or on their own. It's helpful to get all the MFL team to invite at least one student from all their classes. This should give you about ten per cent of the MFL student cohort. In our experience this percentage is important to establish the critical mass.

It is often the case that the language priorities of the MFL team are the same as those of the English department: the ability to speak and write complex sentences requiring connectives and internal punctuation. It is also the case that verb declensions are key to MFL and, where this is the focus, allegiances can be built between staff of the two departments. English teachers tend not to think of the way verbs end quite as explicitly as MFL colleagues. When colleagues share the same aim, for example, to show how verbs change according to tense, we find students saying, 'We did this in English' or 'We did this in German.'

We set a research task for students, asking them: how many different ways are there, in English, of using the phrase: 'to run'? More often than not, they have never thought about it. Ask them: 'Can you each think of a different way of saying this word?' Of course, next lesson, there are many repeats, but they are astonished at the many different ways the infinitive can be declined: *Running, ran, run, runs, will run, has run, could run, might run,* and so on.

Putting it into practice

Ask colleagues in the MFL team two questions:

- What would most help you teach your subject disciplines?
- How do you think you could help us teach English?

MFL colleagues tend to respond with knowledge about core grammar skills, for example an awareness of language about language (such as noun, verb, subject, object) and the ways in which punctuation is similar to English.

Invite the students that the MFL teachers have as literacy leaders to meet with you over four tutor times. Let them know you will inform their parents that they have volunteered to improve standards at the school and that they will be leaders, and can use this recognition in future Personal Statements and so on. Also, with the national agenda being focused on literacy, student leadership of literacy can only help.

Ask the literacy leaders to talk to their language teachers about what skills are going to be taught next in the scheme of work. Encourage student MFL literacy leaders to draw on what they know from their English language learning.

Invite students to explain the use of 'some' or 'any' in English with their French equivalents:

- *du* before a *masculine* word, e.g., *Je mange du pain le matin.* (I have [some] bread for breakfast.)
- *de la* before a *feminine* word, e.g., *Vous avez de la salade?* (Do you have any lettuce?)
- *de l'* before a *singular* word beginning with a *vowel* or *silent h*, e.g., *Tu bois de l'eau?* (Are you drinking [some] water?); *Ma mère a acheté de l'huile.* (My mother bought some oil.)
- *des* before a word in the *plural* form, *e.g., Nous mangeons des légumes.* (We eat [some] vegetables.)

Ask students to do some research with their verbs and make their class curious about how many words in French are so similar to so many in English.

Taking it further

- Invite MFL student literacy leaders to translate key connectives in English with those in French. In a few key strokes, they will find: 'However' translates as: *toutefois, cependant*; e.g., 'However, the recession is not over yet' is *Toutefois, la récession n'est pas encore terminée*.

- Ask students to prepare a ten-minute lesson on a precise form of declension, for example: past to present. It is astounding to see students seize this challenge and capture their peers' attention with the resultant product: be it a spoken and whiteboard-based lesson to a carefully designed 'Prezi' or blog. It is worth discussing for a few minutes how effective the learning experience has been. And, since we are in the business of learning about learning, having students think about peer-to-peer learning further embeds the content of the lesson.

What the students say

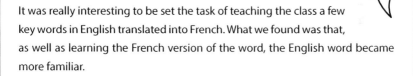

It was really interesting to be set the task of teaching the class a few key words in English translated into French. What we found was that, as well as learning the French version of the word, the English word became more familiar.

Julia, Year 9

What the staff say

We talked with the English department about what sort of connectives were important. The English team gave us a list and we tried to incorporate these into our schemes of work. Sometimes both departments had the time to teach these words within the same fortnight, with obvious benefits.

Linda, French teacher

Strategy 11 'The perfect piece': how having one a term can help progression

Getting started

Accuracy is important, clearly. The aim is to combine this with the energy of innovation and imagination. You must also not discourage students. However, whatever their level of ability, at least one more skill can be achieved.

So, you should say to the students in their English classes: 'At the end of this term, you will each produce one perfect piece of writing. There will be complete spelling, grammar and punctuation accuracy. It will be about a page long in your exercise book. It can be about anything you like. You might choose a story or explanation, or persuasive form. Whatever most interests you and anyone you define as the audience.'

Putting it into practice

Set a reasonable timescale, for example, ten weeks. Return to the piece, periodically, in class or as homework. Give students a minimum and maximum word limit: we found that 50 words as minimum and 500 as maximum works for the purposes of differentiation.

Start with free write. Tell the students that the first drafts are important for content. It is only after the third free write that they will focus on technical accuracy. It's like making a product in design and technology: you draft out ideas, try different versions and only later, polish, sand, paint or varnish the work.

You could show a variety of writers' drafts, for instance an early draft of *Nicholas Nickleby* by Charles Dickens (http://www.bl.uk/onlinegallery/onlineex/englit/nickleby/large17440.html.) It's important for students to see the mistakes, crossings out, changes that even such an internationally-acknowledged author needed. Another example that you mind find helpful is http://internetshakespeare.uvic.ca/Annex/Texts/Ham/Q1/default/. This site allows students and teachers to see the many changes that such an iconic piece of writing as Hamlet went through.

Alternatively, invite a writer into school who is prepared to show his/her early notebooks and then the final published version. You could also invite a publishing editor to describe how he or she takes what the writer has produced and helps him or her perfect it for publication.

Of course, the use of IT writing programmes helps this process. Tell students to set the grammar and spelling checker on the computer as this allows them to see that the programme helps the writer correct mistakes. Do not shy away from the notion of mistake and correction. Again, it is important and interesting to allow students to debate the notion of absolutes in language. They may come to the currently accepted position that language is a contested, socially, industrially defined construct.

Taking it further

Invite students to give a ten-minute lesson on the etymology of any commonly used word or phrase: this is made so much easier with the access to such sites as Wikipedia where the origin of words such as 'hamburger', 'internet' and so on are revealed. The excitement we want you to generate is that all words and grammar rules evolve or legislate into existence. You can lead students into an exploration, for example, of how the Welsh language has become marginalised by political means and that, in the past, to speak or write in Welsh, was deemed worthy of educational sanction. Accessible extracts, for example, from *How Green Was My Valley* by Richard Llewellyn (1939) show how speaking and writing in Welsh was punishable by school rules in surprisingly unacceptable ways.

What the students say

At first it seemed too difficult that I could produce a piece of writing that was "perfect". When the teacher explained that we could take our time, craft and change the writing before Christmas until it was error-free, we felt more reassured. In fact, it made us feel so successful that, when this had been done, we showed it to our parents as an example of what we could do. They were amazed, at least, mine were! The teacher asked us to go back to the writing about once a week and make changes to make it better. We were allowed to use our friends, the teacher, teaching assistant, online grammar and spell checks to get it right. It gave us a sense of doing something important.

Jamie, aged 14

Strategy 12 Bringing connectives to life so that staff feel confident to teach them

Literacy Outcomes

- Staff are made more familiar with the range of ways of linking sentences so that they encourage students to use them.
- Staff know and use the term 'connectives'.

Getting started

Group the connectives into types. We found difference, similarity, extension and flair to be the most effective in terms of widespread usage (see box below). You can present these in the Literacy Box, an online Litbox and/or internet site. The key is to have them widely available and easily accessible. Each school differs but we find all three access points to be valuable.

Different types of connectives

Connectives of difference

However

Although

On the other hand

But

Yet

Still

Nevertheless

Nonetheless

Conversely

Then again

Whereas

Connectives of extension

Furthermore

In addition

What's more

Moreover

Besides

Additionally

Plus

I infer that

We might infer

It is possible to infer

This effect emphasises

This effect highlights

This effect accentuates

This effect underlines

This effect points to

Connectives of flair	Connectives of similarity
It is as if	Similarly
It seems	Likewise
It could be	Also
It is almost as if	Correspondingly
The writer/artist/designer/ scientist suggests	Equally
	In the same way
The writer/artist/designer/ scientist implies	

Putting it into practice

To discover where your main literacy development focus should be, conduct work trawls of perhaps a selection of books drawn from different age and ability groups in the school. Describe the quality of what you find. Share this with your staff.

We focused on writing because in our colleagues' schools, this has been the most disappointing feature of literacy by the end of Year 11. You might note, for instance, how many students cannot write more than simple sentence constructions or, at the higher ability range, some students who find it a challenge to write with nuance, depth of explanation, synthesis and evaluation.

Your next step should be to focus on one or two aspects of writing. Work trawl vertically once a month, again, taking one student from each year group, the sixth named on the cohort register. Brief staff a week before to alert colleagues that they will be asking the students to leave, for one night, all the books in which there is some writing or evidence of reading. Then, on the appointed date, have each student deliver their books to the library or similar open space.

If you are going to do a work trawl with non-specialist staff, and you are focusing on connectives, offer the lists of connectives from the lit box so that colleagues have a shared language with which to discuss what you have found.

Taking it further

- Invite primary partner colleagues in addition to all staff in your school to do this work trawl with you. We had our Head of Year 7 send the invites to our staff and partner colleagues.

- In the library, make a pile of each student's books from across their curriculum range. Supply a simple grid asking two straightforward questions: 'What literacy do you notice that is of high standard?' and 'What literacy do you think needs to be improved?'

What the staff say

It's fascinating to focus in on two or three students from higher, middle and lower ability and see what writing they have achieved, and, via the transition writing, what they are capable of. I also found it helpful to see the type of sentence connectives students can use, what they have used in the past and in other subjects.

Michael, Head of technology

Strategy 13 How to raise confidence by colour-coding literacy

Literacy Outcomes

- A consistent approach to defining key literacy features across the curriculum.
- Student confidence grows because they see the same colour used across all their lessons.
- A more unified approach to the delivery of core literacy skills.
- Staff confidence grows as they know more about what is important to the school and realise there is little extra they have to do in their lessons.

Getting started

Using work trawls and assessment analysis, reveal the key weaknesses and, thus, literacy priorities for the school. For us, this was, across three schools: technical vocabulary; evaluative language; connectives for extended writing; internal punctuation to enable emphasis, detail and nuance.

Putting it into practice

Select the four aspects of text you want to focus on, depending on what has been revealed by assessment and work trawls as generic weaknesses and choose a colour scheme to represent them, (we found that four colours is the most staff and students can cope with). For example, we chose blue for key technical vocabulary, red for evaluative language, green for connectives of all kinds and yellow for internal punctuation. Mark up some exemplar material using the colour scheme and then in a staff meeting, show the exemplar text, introducing the colour scheme and the elements they represent. Then when staff and students are preparing materials that exemplify high quality texts they will feel more confident about identifying the areas that will improve students' writing.

Taking it further

- Ask colleagues to highlight their own exemplar material following the agreed colour scheme.

- Have a student do the presentation to the staff. We had our literacy steering group discuss and agree on the colour coding. We gave them the outcome of the work trawl and assessment findings and they decided on the colours and chose the four key areas for the school.

What the staff say

It was strange to be told we were colour-coding our best writing. And to start with, we didn't really like being told what colours to use and that we all had to use the same pattern…But it works…It worked partly because we complained about it in the staffroom. Talking with others about which colours to use and what a connective was and whether technical language should be blue or red helped us, without our knowing, into the literacy project.

Julia, science teacher

What the students say

I find it helps to see the same colours each time. And by the time you get into Year 9, you know exactly what to expect.

What's good is that teachers are sort of speaking the same language. It's interesting to know that they talk to each other! And it does stop people thinking English is only important in English lessons. We were used to English at primary school being everywhere. But in secondary it isn't. When we saw our teachers talking from the same script, it built our confidence. I find it helps to see the same colours each time.

Danielle, aged 14

Strategy 14 'Each one teach one': improving writing and reading examination questions in technology

Literacy Outcomes

- Improved student confidence with technology-specific language.
- Improved ability to write examination answers.
- Improved ability to identify writing genre.

Getting started

Provide students with typical questions from examination papers in resistant materials. These are high-value questions, attracting significant numbers of marks. Here are a few adapted examples.

- *Use notes and sketches to show how you would develop the design features of your chosen mp3 player with speakers.*
- *Evaluate your developed design.*
- *Give details of a specific process where you would use each tool.*
- *Discuss the possible environmental impact of using plastic to manufacture products.*

Ask students to read through the questions and delete all the words that are unnecessary. This is a key learning moment. Students, in pairs, solo, or groups, reach a variety of preliminary conclusions. Often they say that there are no redundancies; this in itself is a step forwards. It teaches them to read each part of the question carefully.

Next, ask them to rank order, using a highlighter, the words in any one question. Ask: 'What are the top three most important words. Be prepared to argue your case for your choice. You will have only one minute to explain your rank order.'

Again, it's fascinating to see how students' responses are either very similar or completely different. What's key is that there's debate about language and that students are trying to thinking as if they were an examiner.

Putting it into practice

Tell students that they are about to read something critical to their success. Advise them that the activity may be too difficult or that this would usually only be attempted by an older year group or teachers: most student enjoy the feeling that they are being challenged. The activity is in a common training exercise for subject teachers deconstructing exam papers' rhetoric.

To engage curiosity, seal the questions in envelopes. Mark them, for example: 'Essential', 'Key', 'For authorised eyes only'. (Alternatively, you can put the questions in folders in the shared area/VLE.) Place the envelopes around the room. Discuss with the teaching assistant, or think aloud, whether the class should have access to the material in the envelopes, creating a sense of excitement; of course, what you are showing them has been pre-released by the examination board and is freely available, but making them think otherwise makes the activity more engaging.

Taking it further

Ask the class to attempt an answer to the questions. Then set up an in-role 'examiners' standardisation meeting.' Set this up with as much formality as possible. Say, for example: 'Thank you for attending this meeting. We are about to influence the lives of thousands of students throughout the country. You are going to see real answers, written by real students. We would like you to comment on the best answers. If you can, point out how answers could be improved.' Dependent on the examination board, offer grade criteria for the in-role examiners to use. This itself can be a valuable extension activity for some students: to re-write high-grade criteria into 'student speak'.

Have students devise their own questions using the exemplars you've given.

What the staff say

As a further step, you can add a sense of intrigue by marking folders in the VLE 'Restricted access'. I had the IT technician in the room with me while we, in role, debated whether to allow students to open the folders. Of course, before we had finished, some already had. And they scanned the questions with surprise at what was there. They were of course seeing nothing more than what is readily available via the Examination Board's website.

We pretended we were disappointed if anyone gained access to the folders, saying things like: "I thought this was password protected"; "How did they do that?" "Who gave away the username?" We did this with deadpan expressions because older students are pretty good at detecting a set-up.

Of course, at the end of the lesson, we made sure every student left knowing precisely what we had done. It's important none actually thinks they have compromised the school's IT security system or breached our 'Acceptable Use Policy'.

Anne, resistant materials teacher

What the students say

Even though a few teachers use the envelope thing to make a lesson interesting, it does work. The teacher told us it was a set-up, so we knew they weren't doing anything wrong. And when you see an envelope with the words "For your eyes only", of course you want to see what's inside.

The editing exercise is good because it's easier to take words away than to add them. And what was surprising was that there were very few words you could take away from the question and it still made sense. What was more difficult was picking the three most important words.

The activity took about 20 minutes. The teacher kept looking at her watch and telling us the exercise had to be completed on time. "That's part of the examination training," she said, "to keep strictly to a time limit."

James, aged 14

Strategy 15 Agreeing the literacy focus with your staff

Literacy Outcomes

- A database of high-quality writing to which students and parents can reference to improve the quality of their writing.
- An increased sense of students helping to lead literacy. In order to keep the literacy project, the 'literacy village', thriving, students must be co-leaders.
- Staff and students have access to annotated writing indicating high-quality written features.

Getting started

Sometimes you need a very tight focus to get your literacy project started. Have staff prepared and invite them to focus on Year 11. Have them choose and give to you one very high-quality piece of writing either externally or internally moderated. Ask them to choose a genre of writing that will make a difference to any grade boundary with which they are most concerned.

We found this highly instructive to do as an English departmental meeting exercise. After all, team meetings should be about improving the quality of learning rather than administration. All that can be done my email or conversation.

Putting it into practice

Break staff into pairs and ask them to take two pieces of cross-departmental writing each. Indicate by using margin notes, highlighting and arrows, any excellent use of a few key language features. You could choose, for example, connectives, internal punctuation, use of subject-specific vocabulary – or any features that you have identified by work trawling as key weaknesses across the school.

After the meeting, colour-scan the texts and give them back to the departmental teams through the intranet Litbox, VLE, and as laminates for the Literacy Box so that they can be used at home and school. In an assembly, show students where these subject-specific exemplars have been stored, how they could get access to them and how to use them. Invite volunteer students to show how easy it is to reach each of the access points.

Taking it further

In these assemblies show students how to teach their class about the language features that have made the writing high quality. This takes a few assemblies but is well worth it. Start by asking, questions like:

- What makes great teaching?
- How do you remember what you have been told?
- What makes great writing?

Students will invariably reply that they like to be involved; they like clear explanations; they can't cope with too much at any one time and they like focus. These become the guidelines for students volunteering for your literacy leadership programme.

What the students say

We don't often get shown what makes good writing outside English so it's good to know where we could see it and for every subject. The pieces of writing aren't that long and some are only extracts. But you can easily see where the writer has done well with things like punctuation.

In our Year group, Thursday is literacy day. Every Thursday morning we do one of the following three things: read silently, fiction or non-fiction; our literacy leaders show us a PowerPoint or Prezi format from the Literacy Box, or we write an entry in our "Learning Log".

This is part of our Student Planner. We write about which lessons we learned a lot from or how we can learn better. Then we discuss these in pairs. Sometimes, we divide the tutor group in half. Half of us swap into another tutor group and pair up, sharing how we learn best with someone we wouldn't usually meet. This means we might come across a technique like singing or writing a poem about a scientific formula to remember it better.

Nathan, aged 15

What the staff say

It was reassuring that all we had to do was to find a single piece
of writing, give it to the English department and we got back a
hard copy and e-version with annotations that helped us as a department to
recognise high-quality writing.

I even tried having a member of my class describe this text to her peers. All
it took was a simple preparatory exercise. I asked the literacy leader to find the
example geography text in the Literacy Box and get ready to describe it the
following week.

I was surprised at how easily the student took up the challenge. She had
a partner to work with so it wasn't so daunting. But the effect was pleasing.
To have the class paying more attention to a student than they do to me was
fascinating.

Deborah, geography teacher

Strategy 16 How to demonstrate cross-curricular writing types

Literacy Outcomes

- Students and staff have access to types of writing they may need.
- Students' literacy leadership is improved by introducing or teaching these styles to their peers.

Getting started

Have a student literacy leader upload to the whiteboard, the style example you wish to exemplify. Show how this style is relevant to the writing assignment needed in the lesson. At the end of this strategy is an extensive list of different styles, example material and the effect of the style for you to use for this strategy.

Putting it into practice

Tell the students that in this lesson they will need to read and write in a particular style. Show the style, its example and effect from the exemplars provided at the end of this strategy. It is important for the students to know what the examiner expects to see. But, more importantly, it helps students understand how to write for and persuade, real audiences.

Taking it further

- Produce the text styles, effects and exemplars as laminated strips.
- As the students arrive in your lesson, hand them a strip. On it is written the name of a style. Then have the students tell each other what they have been given and how it might connect to the subject.
- Invite students to explain the style to a partner.

- Display signs in each of the four corners of your room such as: 'Diary'; 'Newspaper'; 'Scientific report'; 'Geography textbook'. Have the students move to the text type that best fits with the style they have been given. The learning occurs when students talk to each other and/or discuss with one another where their style best fits. The point is that you get students thinking explicitly about styles of language and what they might achieve. Make it clear that there are, probably, no wrong answers: 'If you take your factual writing style to the 'Diary' corner, you may well be right. If you take your emotive style to the 'Geography textbook' corner, you might well be able to give a good explanation for this. Sometimes, students change their mind once they have reached their text type and tried to justify their decision. Again, the key point is, that if they change their mind, they are making progress.

What the students say

I found it really helpful to have this simple sheet available on the school's VLE. I could stick it to my exercise book as an example of what the teacher and examiner needed.

When we were given the text types as we came into the classroom, we wondered what was going on. The teacher said, that's what she needed, for us to be curious about language.

We had to tell each other what text type we had been given. And then we had one minute to write one sentence in the same style, then explain it to a partner.

It was difficult but interesting to say whether we would need personal or impersonal language in the lesson. For geography, I remember, we said it might be a bit of both but probably impersonal [language] because it looked like that's how our books were written.

The teacher asked us why personal [language] might not work. I remember thinking after a few minutes discussion about whether personal style might be better. After all, what we know about the world around us has been the result of people's discoveries. So, why not use a personal style? We had a class talk about that and some people could see the link between language and discovering things. When we did the "move toward the text-type corner" exercise, people had real difficulty making their minds up. But they felt OK after we were told that if we think there is more than one answer, this is a sign of thinking and learning.

Simon, aged 14

What the staff say

We put these exemplars on the school's VLE and intranet. It was also on the school's internet resource, the Litweb. So, parents and students could see what we meant when we said we wanted them to write in a subjective, personal or formal manner. The 'bite-size' nature of these examples helped students and staff overcome the worry of using the resource.

I asked the students to say which type of writing would be most effective. This only took a few minutes. And I don't have more than that because there's so much content to deliver.

Julie, religious education teacher

Text types, exemplars and effects

Style: Formal
Example: The way the planets are structured gives rise to gravitational pull
Effect: Believable, thoughtful, ordered, can disguise an opinion

Style: Informal
Example: Oi, see these planets, right? They spin like anything.
Effect: Chatty, colloquial, friendly, easy to relate to, makes it sound like an opinion, like someone's talking to you

Style: Personal
Example: When I first saw the planets they made me feel awed and humble
Effect: Draws the reader to the writer, biased, makes it sound like an opinion

Style: Impersonal
Example: The planets spin on their axes and have strong gravitational pull
Effect: Cold, believable, distances reader and writer

Style: Factual
Example: It takes seven seconds for the light to travel from the sun, even at a speed of 186,000 miles per second
Effect: Credible, authoritative, truthful, unbiased

Style: Emotive
Example: The small, isolated, frozen little planets float silently in the endless dark
Effect: Makes the reader feel things, helps the reader understand the feelings of the writer, helps the reader identify with the writer

Style: Descriptive or adjectival
Example: Mars has a deep, red glow and its surface is barren, dry and cold
Effect: Makes a text descriptive, visual, detailed, can be biased

Style: Non-adjectival
Example: Mars' surface cannot support life
Effect: Colder, more scientific, less biased

Style: Figurative
Example: Brilliant teardrops on the face of the sky
Effect: Emotive, rich, descriptive, detailed, personal, biased

Style: Referential
Example: The planets are above us in the sky and do not emit their own light
Effect: Seems unbiased (but might not be), straightforward, seems truthful

Style: Objective
Example: There is no life on any planets, according to the SETI listening survey
Effect: Seems truthful, seems unbiased

Style: Subjective
Example: I believe there must be life on one of the moons of Jupiter
Effect: Seems biased, full of the writer's opinions

Style: Passive (No pronouns *I, he, she, you, we*)
Example: It has been said that there is no life on any of the other planets
Effect: Seems truthful, credible, believable

Style: Active (Plenty of pronouns)
Example: I know there is no life on any other worlds
Effect: Makes it seem like an opinion, more personal

Style: Diction patterns
Example: Deadly vacuum drawing all light away from the sun/ Night has no mercy, it is the enemy of the stars/ the planets are the lost children of the galaxy.
Effect: Creates a mood or an atmosphere. The diction pattern is: cold, forbidding, empty, vast; it helps you see what the writer's attitude is: that space is a frightening, almost an aggressive place

Style: First person
Example: I, we, my, mine, me
Effect: Involving, immediate, intimate

Style: Second person
Example: You, yours, you're
Effect: By using the second person, a writer can directly address and thus involve the reader in the text.

Style: Third person
Example: He, she, they, it
Effect: Can make it seem more certain or definite about who did what

Style: Standard English
Example: Unidentified flying objects have been seen landing and taking off in the silent places of Warwickshire
Effect: Seems truthful, believable, seems unbiased

Style: Non-standard English
Example: It's brill and groovy, these wicked UFOs are like all over the shop, innit
Effect: Seems less truthful, lacks credibility, biased

Style: Sentence type: Command
Example: Look up into the sky and you will see the night come alive
Effect: Puts the writer in a position of power

Style: Sentence type: Question
Example: Would you leave the earth to travel beyond the stars?
Effect: Involves reader; also doubtful, unsure, uncertain

Style: Sentence type: Statement
Example: It is impossible to travel in time
Effect: Definite, sure, certain

Style: Sentence type: Exclamation
Example: If matter meets anti-matter the whole place will explode!
Effect: Exciting, emotional, urgent

Style: Fragmented syntax
Example: It's like, well, I don't know, awesome…I can't think of the word, something – no, it's beyond me
Effect: Uncertain, emotional

Style: Controlled syntax
Example: We want to travel into the distant night because we are born to explore. Our minds are not content to rest easy on the earth. Space is there for us to make our new home.
Effect: Ordered, thoughtful, calm

Style: Simile
Example: The moon is like a huge white balloon
Effect: Comparing two similar ideas/objects/feelings using the words *as* or *like* to create an image

Style: Metaphor
Example: The moon is a huge white balloon
Effect: Giving the characteristics of one idea/object/feeling to another to create an image

Style: Personification
Example: The rain pounded on the window
Effect: Giving human characteristics to something that is non-human in order to create an image

Style: Anthropomorphism

Example: The eagle watched with anticipation

Effect: Giving human characteristics to an animal, giving the reader a better understanding of its thoughts and feelings

Style: Onomatopoeia

Example: The pots and pans clanged together in a chorus of plinking and plonking

Effect: Words that sound like the noise they make, creating sound images

Style: Alliteration

Example: She nearly knocked her niece over

Effect: Words that start with the same sound coming close together in a sentence, to emphasise a point or highlight a feeling

Style: Assonance

Example: Snug as a bug in a rug

Effect: Repetition of similar vowel sounds in words close together, to mimic a certain noise or to emphasise a point

Style: Consonance

Example: He stabbed her and grabbed bag

Effect: Repetition of similar consonant sounds in words close together, to mimic a certain noise or to emphasise a point

Style: Aural imagery

Example: The cork popped out and the fizzy drink sploshed into the glass

Effect: Words and phrases used to create sound images

Style: Imagery

Example: Swooping and souring through the sky the birds cried out in a chorus of song

Effect: Words and phrases used to create visual images

Style: Symbolism

Example: It was summer. Blue skies, hot sun, happy thought. Their relationship seemed to take on a new meaning

Effect: Using an object, theme or image to represent something else

Style: Ambiguity

Example: Perch on their water-perch

Effect: Confuses the reader and makes the meaning unclear

Strategy 17 How to design a 'Litweb'

Literacy Outcomes

- Standards in terms of expected levels of progress in literacy can improve, especially in the focus areas you have identified.
- A more effective home/school partnership.
- An excitement from students that their learning materials might be used by their immediate community and, possibly an international audience.

Getting started

The phrase 'functional skills' has a resonance beyond school and we wanted to show governors and employers that the Litweb we were developing had currency in the world of work.

We confined the contents of our Litweb to *Writing*, *Reading* and *Speaking and Listening*. When visitors clicked on any one of these buttons, they were taken to a content list of resources and one more click allowed them access to student-made, teacher-checked resources.

One of our students invented a site that can be found at: www.chenderit.info/litweb.

Putting it into practice

Invite students to create a literacy support website. It is astonishing what students can find to help them develop simple but effective websites.

Brief students that, within three clicks of logging on, a visitor should be able to get to a useable resource. Also explain that you want simplicity and ease of use. Say that you want to be able to use this site at parents' evenings, staff meetings and any other public event. Of course, it must be linked to the school's secure VLE. Motivate students by saying that their materials could be accessed by a global audience.

Students have to be sure their web-based materials are high quality. This means checking by the teachers. However, it's an important lesson for students that not everything gets published.

Taking it further

Using exemplar resources that have been developed by members of your school community has greater currency than 'off-the-shelf materials'. It seems that, in the spirit of the 'literacy village' co-constructed resources provoke interest. It certainly inspires students with the idea that they can get to reach a potentially international audience.

It is important that you use every possible avenue to bring helpful resources to as wide an audience as possible. You should ensure that the same resources are available in the following four places:

- The physical Literacy Box, containing easy-to-use literacy laminates.
- The intranet Litbox containing the same resources in the Literacy Box.
- A school VLE site, called Litbox that the school's community can use, again replicating what exists physically and in electronic form.
- The internet site, Litweb, which allows access to a global audience. The difference between the two is that the Litweb is accessible by anyone because it's an internet site whereas the Litbox is accessible only to the school community. So, for example, some students are more willing to post images of their writing on the intranet site rather than have it available to wider audience.

You may find it useful to develop an 'editorial board' that ensures the accuracy of the materials students are writing for the various platforms. This work is too much for one member of staff, so consider developing a 'Literacy steering group' which could be around 15 volunteer students from across the Year groups and two staff. They could meet once a half-term and divide up between them the resources that have been made submitted over the last six weeks. It should then take only about an hour to go through them and make corrections where necessary. Alternatively, try using an A-level language class and an A-level media class as the editorial board. They are good at seeing basic errors and it is valuable learning to have the class discuss the various effectiveness of what has been produced.

What the students say

It was really good to feel that we had made a resource that could be used around the world. To make teaching materials useful for people we'll never meet is exciting. It's what the internet is about when it works well. We liked designing a site that could be used by students, parents and even teachers.

James, aged 14

What the staff say

It is so helpful to know that students in my class can access literacy resources while I teach. I can direct parents to the internet site. It was especially impressive to have students come into our staff briefings and show us what they had made and how to use it. The most persuasive thing was hearing students whose confidence and competence had grown as a result of accessing and/or making literacy resources. My colleagues felt reassured because the resources had been checked by English staff. It was good to know that we could continue with our subject content while literacy leaders showed the class how to use connectives, internal punctuation or paragraphing. Somehow, when they listen to their peers, the class paid especial attention.

Karen, history teacher

Links to other strategies

- Strategy 4 'How to design a Literacy Box' on page 31.
- Strategy 8 'How to set up a literacy steering group' on page 41.

Strategy 18 How to use staff briefing sessions to promote literacy

Literacy Outcomes

- A constant, consistent focus on the literacy project.
- Staff feel informed.
- Staff have the opportunity to try out a strategy that day.
- Standards gains. The more you repeat a message in different ways, the more likely it is to stick and to lead to a natural way of teaching and learning.

Getting started

Most schools have a morning briefing session once a week. Some are lucky enough to have two a week, each lasting ten minutes. If you don't have this, try to persuade colleagues that this is an excellent way to get general news and, especially, to deliver training to your colleagues.

You can call these sessions whatever you wish. It is a form of micro-training: highly intense, early in the day and iterative.

Putting it into practice

Plan the year. If, say, you have one ten-minute information meeting a week, that's 39 times to reinforce the message. And because these sessions tend to be quite brief, the strategy you want to reinforce or suggest is in more of a 'digestible bite-size'. We found that, in a compressed form, staff often take in more and even want more.

Use the time you have to showcase literacy, through reinforcement, question and answer. Ask students to lead and give feedback, or to demonstrate the progress they have made through a particular strategy. This is especially effective when students show the literacy learning materials they have made and has the added advantage that, properly prepared, the student literacy leaders will model the kind of interaction you want. This is all part of developing the 'literacy village', self-sustaining, outward looking, innovative, evolutionary.

Ask students to introduce to the staff a connective or punctuation mark that staff might find intriguing. As odd as it may seem, words like 'moreover' and 'nevertheless' will get staff thinking how they could include these in their teaching. Punctuation such as the ellipsis also seems to provoke interest.

Taking it further

- When we said above, 'plan the year's 'micro-training', this doesn't mean you have to plan 39 entirely different areas of literacy input. It is likely that your work trawls and assessment information have shown there are two or three high leverage areas.

What the students say

It was nerve-wracking to stand up in front of the whole staff but I was in a group so that made it easier. I felt a real sense of achievement when we'd finished. And staff kept come up to me in the day to say how well I'd done. It was good that we got a chance to tell teachers what helped us. We felt we had a voice and had been listened to.

Some staff asked me and my partner to come into their lesson and give a ten-minute lesson. We were only allowed to do six a year. And we really enjoyed it. The teacher would keep the class under control so we could share the material we had made and ask questions of the class. It is good that we only had ten minutes. I don't think we could have kept going for longer.

Jason, aged 13

Strategy 19 How to use literacy as a thinking starter

Literacy Outcomes

- Students improve their knowledge of language to help them think creatively and openly.
- Students improve their thinking skills.
- The whole-school questioning ethos is helped: it is so important that teachers and students ask questions of each other and about the content of their learning.

Getting started

Suggest to staff that they can use these thinking phrases and verbs as lesson starters. Suggest that they can train their students or literacy leaders to help lead their use.

Make the resources available as an invitation. Suggest to staff that this will take very little time to use, especially if they use their literacy leaders.

Of course, try the strategy with a small group of staff to begin with. Then have the relevant students and staff explain how they made use of them and what benefits were secured. These testimonies are the most effective.

Prepare the Bloom's thinking phrases (at the end of this strategy) as laminates in the Litbox or Litweb.

Putting it into practice

Access an image website such as www.worth1000.com. Choose any publicly available image; there will be many that interest you. We found that choosing an image that has no obvious connection to the lesson content can be the most valuable. What you want to do is encourage curiosity, inventiveness and imagination. Display the image on your whiteboard as the students come into the classroom. Ask them to guess what the image has to do with what they have learned in the previous lesson to build on prior learning.

Now, choose a thinking genre on which you wish to focus. Have your Bloom's laminates, taken from the Literacy Box, face down on the students' desks. Or you can have them ready on the intranet. You can, technology willing, click between the curiosity image and the thinking phrase/word group as you wish. We found this to be highly effective when you say to students, something like: 'You have ten seconds to memorise as many phrases/word as you can.' If the texts are laminated, say something like 'You have ten seconds to turn over the cards and memorise as many words/phrases as you can.'

Have students predict what the links might be between the current lesson content and the image you used as a starter. Invite the students to use as many of the thinking words and phrases in their discussion. It doesn't matter if they get it wrong. In fact, this is key. We need to help students use the thinking registers without fear of failure; so praise an attempt at experimentation and then model how the language can be used effectively.

Keep showing the thinking texts to students so they become more familiar with them. The key is to stimulate curiosity rather than create stress. Most students enjoy the challenge of capturing as much high-quality language as they can.

Taking it further

- Choose students who will lead the presentation of a group of Bloom's phrases. The students could be your literacy leaders. We found it helpful to have the students distribute the texts to their peers, leading the starter. They asked their peers to say a sentence that contained the words they had been given.

- You can invite the class to say which Bloom's group will be most useful in the lesson. It's fascinating to have this discussion. In a science lesson about photosynthesis, for example, it is a highly effective literacy/thinking starter to have students choose between the syntheses register and the evaluation register. The learning is in the discussion and dispute.

- Have students add more words and phrases to a group of phrases and words. It doesn't matter if they get this wrong: again, the point is to encourage experimentation with language.

What the students say

At the start, we wondered what was going on. Why were we being shown a picture that seemed to have no connection with what we were doing? But it was interesting to have the teacher say that we were being challenged to make links. I really like this. So often we just turn up to a lesson and listen to the teacher. I like being asked to say what the lesson might be about.

Jemma, aged 15

What the staff say

Having the thinking phrases in the Litbox and in the Litweb made it really easy to put them in front of the class. And I liked being told that we could use these or not as we felt appropriate. What puts staff off is being told to do something. It's much better being shown by fellow staff and/or students that they have gained from a particular strategy. I enjoyed seeing students' curiosity as they saw the group of words and phrases projected onto the whiteboard. So I took this one step further. As the students came into the classroom, I had a student hand out, to everyone, a laminated phrase or word from the taxonomy. It's great that, from the first minute of the lesson, students are being challenged and made to ask how this language might help them. We find that students get very possessive over the language laminate they have been given and want to try it out in a question to the teacher.

This can happen in a hot-seating session, for example. I tried being in role as "light". Students were invited to ask me what I did, what I might link to, how valuable I was, how I might work and so on. I started the hot-seating by saying that we only had five minutes to get ten questions asked. Another student timed the starter. The result: pace and innovation and exploration of this key science content. And I have used this in many other new content topics. I find that students enjoy challenging the teacher and trying to catch me out.

Lisa, PHSE teacher in Year 10

Bloom's thinking phrases

Knowledge:
- list, define, tell, describe, identify, show, label, collect, examine, tabulate, quote, name, who, when, where.

Comprehension
- summarise, describe, interpret, contrast, predict, associate, distinguish, estimate, differentiate, discuss, extend.

Application
- apply, demonstrate, calculate, complete, illustrate, show, solve, examine, modify, relate, change, classify, experiment, discover.

Analysis
- analyse, separate, order, explain, connect, classify, arrange, divide, compare, select, explain, infer.

Synthesis
- combine, integrate, modify, rearrange, substitute, plan, create, design, invent, what is it?, compose, formulate, prepare, generalise, rewrite assess, decide, rank, grade, test, measure, recommend, convince, select, judge, explain, discriminate, support, conclude, compare.

Innovation
- what if, supposing, say, let's say, imagine, picture, envisage, visualise, see in your mind's eye, think of, consider, conceive of, create in your mind.

Strategy 20 How to encourage boys' writing

Literacy Outcomes

- Boys are engaged in writing activities through digital media.
- Boys are inspired to research their favourite films and books.
- Boys recommend writing to one another.

Getting started

Colleagues sometimes say that they need a strategy to help raise boys' interest in literacy. This strategy has been of use to such colleagues.

There is great benefit in approaching writing through an oblique method: in this case, using digital media.

Invite a class of underachieving boys to transform their English class into a television station. Allow them to pick a name, our group chose 'Eyewitness News'. At least one lesson a week, turn the classroom into a television studio. You could even link up a digital camera to a television monitor. This would enable those not in front of the camera to direct, instruct and explain what was happening in the broadcast.

Make it clear that, if it is good enough, the media product will be shown to the rest of the school, possibly on large screen, at lunchtime in the school cafeteria.

Putting it into practice

When you have decided on your focus, tell them how to become a television company for the school. Ask them to think of what sort of audience they would they like to broadcast to. Students may query whether anyone will watch their programme. Explain to them that, the more attractive they can make their literacy product the more peer students will pay some sort of attention. Television isn't something people have to watch; they must be persuaded to give their attention.

Consider inviting local TV news stations to give you recent scripts of news broadcasts. You will find, as we did, that they are only too willing to participate, especially if you emphasise that their participation is in the interests of whole-school and community literacy. Analyse with the boys the way the scripts are written so that they can write them themselves. The students might be a little daunted by some of the technical jargon, but scripts are generally designed for maximum efficiency and therefore contain only the text that is needed.

Using the news genre allows a fixed camera position and, therefore, minimal cutting and editing. The students show their news edit to their own class and, where the quality is strong enough, to their year group peers in an assembly.

Taking it further

- Set a camera up linked to a TV monitor. Describe a seemingly simple sequence. The one we use is as follows: A student comes into an empty room. He or she sees a pound coin on the floor. He or she checks that the room is empty. He or she picks up the coin. He or she exits the room. The students behind the camera direct the sequence. Since this requires no sound, they can talk over the recording and thus shape the direction of the scene. When you play it back, use mute. Keep the scenario to about five minutes as this will mean students are more likely to engage. Encourage students to appreciate the detailed thinking that goes into the construction of even such a simple sequence.

- We vary the 'coin narrative' by suggesting it is filmed as a mystery genre, soap opera genre or news genre. The oracy that results is invariably fascinating and leads to students asking if they can see exemplar scripts that create such genre. This is, of course, exactly what you want: student curiosity, especially that focused on written text.

- Discuss how a scene might be filmed: who might be in the fore and background; whether there might be a close up of a face, a wound, or a weapon. Such are the almost limitless possibilities, reading the text becomes a vehicle for imagining film interpretation.

- You could also use shots of the death of Mercutio in Lurman's *Romeo and Juliet*. The script for this is available online at: http://sfy.ru/?script=romeo_and_juliet_96_ts

Excerpt of text from Romeo and Juliet

BENVOLIO
Art thou hurt?

MERCUTIO
Ay, ay, a scratch, a scratch. Ay, a scratch, a scratch. HA HA HA.

ROMEO
Courage man, the hurt cannot be much.

MERCUTIO
'Twill serve. Ask for me tomorrow and you shall find
me a grave man. A plague o' both your houses. They
have made worms meat of me. A plague on both your
Houses! Why the devil did you come between us? I was
hurt under your arm.

ROMEO
I thought all for the best.

MERCUTIO
A Plague o' both your houses.

ROMEO
NO! Mercutio!

It works to have this script extract in sealed envelopes and offered as reward for high-quality oracy having seen the film sequence. Again, what you are after is curiosity about text. The students want to see what has been concealed. Eventually allow them to read it.

- Set the students the assignment to research film scripts. They can cut and paste short extracts for use in class. They share their thoughts as to the filmic realisation of such extracts.

- Ask students to name their favourite films. Sometimes these will be interpretations of novels and plays. Students feel empowered when they search through any search engine for copyright-protected film scripts. They live their lives more through the visual media than print. What's encouraging for them is that behind each visual presentation is a text-based narrative.

We often find students surprised, to say the least, by the fact that the actors are following a written script.

- Students can be encouraged by seeing the pitch, the treatment, the early drafts and the final script of a film or TV show they know.

What the staff say

What made this work was a number of things: we weren't reading for its own sake, there was an end purpose that caught the interest and attention of the class; the texts we read were to help us create our own programme. And there was a sense that we were a television company, rather than a class.

Jennifer, English teacher

Strategy 21 How to help art students improve their use of paragraphs

Literacy Outcomes

- Improved evaluative writing.
- Student engagement with the learning process.
- High leverage work for the teacher: they don't have to do a great deal for a significant standards gain.

Getting started

In GCSE Art, a key writing feature is accurate self-evaluation of students' work. Here the Literacy Box and the intranet Litbox can be key. When students see the types of connectives they can use and the teacher models their use, there's a better chance of high-quality output.

In particular, when staff can find a model text and use it to demonstrate what high-standard writing looks like, this encourages emergent writers. Even more helpful is using writing that has been produced by students known to the class. Invite writers who are regarded as 'cool' to contribute to the Litweb. Of course, this changes year to year. But peer exemplars are significantly influential.

Putting it into practice

Ask your Head of art for a copy of an exceptional evaluative piece of writing. This can be writing from a student at your school or a standardised GCSE Board supplied extract.

Offer the following to your English team as a training exercise. Have English colleagues annotate the writing, highlighting:

- Connectives.
- Internal punctuation (commas, colons, semi colons).
- High-value specialist vocabulary.

This often works with an agreed colour code so the school gets used to recognising key linguistic features.

Offer the writing back to the art team as a pdf. The advantage is that they have had to do nothing except select high-quality writing, and the English team will get to see and help improve writing outside their curriculum area.

Taking it further

Invite the art team to select two or three students who will help lead the teaching of this exemplar writing. Students enjoy being asked to an English team meeting to learn the features of high-standard writing. Generally they feel more comfortable in a group and this has obvious advantages in terms of expanding the number of students who see themselves as leaders of literacy.

Remember this project is about co-construction. Literacy across the curriculum has a much better chance of becoming part of the school's 'DNA' when students feel some ownership of the process.

What the students say

I liked being in an English Department meeting. The teachers treated me really well. They even gave me biscuits. I felt like a bit of a celebrity. They asked me to sit where I wanted. I was glad I had my friend! We sat with the teachers and they treated me as one of them. We talked about how we could point out the good things in the writing. It was easier than I thought. And I really enjoyed teaching to my art class. There was less hassle than I thought. The writing was there in the Literacy Box and all I had to do was point out where the best examples were. It was strange having all the class looking at me but my teacher said I got more attention that she did!'

Natasha, Year 10

I was struck by the idea of a 'literacy village'. I wanted to be part of it. I hoped that my evaluation writing would be included in the VLE. Of course, I didn't tell anyone, but my art teacher told me that my writing had been used as an example of good practice within the whole school. I was so proud. Then I was asked into a staff morning briefing to tell the teachers what had helped me.

Basically it came down to being shown ways of writing that I could use. Phrases such as: *'It is as if...' 'It would be...' 'I hoped to imply...' 'I wanted to suggest...' 'I wanted to foreground...' 'I wanted the viewer to...' 'imply/think/feel/act...'*

What I think is: art is is about making things happen in people's hearts, minds and the way they behave. What was so useful was to be given the phrases that could help me do that.

Jane, Year 12

What the staff say

It was so much more manageable knowing that the students would take a lead. And having writing that had been produced by students in the school was so helpful. It's the connection between students and their aspirations that is encouraged. When they see writing that has come from our school, it makes it so much easier to ask students: "Why shouldn't it be you that writes like this?"

Too often students think the best quality writing is produced elsewhere by people outside their experience.

We had discussed as a staff the concept of the "literacy village" and this struck a chord with myself and my colleagues. Students need to see an immediate connection between themselves and excellent writing.

Anna, art teacher

Strategy 22 How 'Plenary Leaders' can help improve communication skills

> ## Literacy Outcomes
>
> - Improvement in student relationships with each other and with staff.
> - Improvement in student understanding of learning.
> - Improvement in the culture of whole-school leadership.
> - Introducing the notion of 'praise phrase' into the assessment for learning moments and the mid- or end-lesson plenaries.

Getting started

This strategy came about as a result of making use of the fact that inevitably, one's lessons are going to be interrupted on occasion. The key is to make this a virtue. So, we invented a number of literacy-based behavioural characteristics that we wanted students to show. These are context specific. The effectiveness of this strategy is its focus on what each school needs. You choose the behaviours you most want to prioritise across the school and the forms of speaking that you most want to emphasise. Each of these is turned into a 'leadership playing card' and these are duplicated in colleagues' Literacy Box and Litweb.

Putting it into practice

Start by deciding which behavioural characteristics you most wish to improve. Our experience has been that by focusing on the literacy of assessment for learning, greetings and so on (they are listed over the page), students are more likely to internalise the behaviours you wish to improve.

In all ten literacy behaviours or leadership roles (below), you need to teach students the discourse markers of politeness and courtesy. So, with, for example, 'the greeter', say: 'Calisha, when someone comes into the classroom, you stand up and courteously say: "Welcome to our class. Can I tell you what we're learning today?" Your visitor will not decline such an invitation.' Calisha continues: What we're learning is...' And she refers to the learning objectives you have posted. The effects are significant, for example:

- The rest of the class pays attention to Calisha's courteous language.

- The class is reminded of the learning objectives.

- Your visitor is impressed with the quality of polite language used.

- The class gives a short applause to the greeter.

All this takes about two minutes.

Another example would be 'the assessor':

- Give permission to up to three students to get up, whenever they like, and check the quality of learning in the class.

- Teach the assessors discourse markers such as: 'Do you think you are making progress today?'; 'Do you think you are making "rapid progress" today?'

- Then, at your mid-lesson or end-lesson plenary, ask your assessors to feedback to the class. Ask them questions like: 'What have you noticed today?'

By and large, your students will be more positive than you might think. But occasionally, and helpfully, they will be uncertain as to what progress has been made or what, indeed 'progress' means for an individual student. This gives you an opportunity to talk about what progress means and what it means for individual students. Clearly, you do this with care, choosing as your examples those students who will benefit from having their learning made public.

Below are the ten literacy behaviours we needed to improve in our schools. It is, of course, up to you to decide which oracy behaviours will have the most effective impact in your school.

The Assessor Use the DLOs and or level descriptors to find any good or exceptional progress.
The Chair Make sure everyone is included, listens well and keep to time.
The Questioner Ask at least three open questions and two closed questions: *wh and h.*
The Greeter If a guest comes to the room, greet them, welcome them and ask if you can tell them what we are learning today.

The Celebrator In the plenary, find two examples of people working well together or producing high quality learning.
The Literacy Coordinator Find any two examples of people using high quality language.
The Learning to Learn Assessor Find any two examples of people learning well: how were they doing this?
The Target Leader Ask any three people how close they are to their personal target.
The Numeracy Coordinator Find two examples of people using numbers well.
The Emotional Literacy Leader What emotions were important today?

Taking it further

Ask the students to invent the leadership roles; this can be a highly-effective way of engaging them in self-regulation. Sometimes they will come up with a few fascinating roles. We found students coming up with titles such as: 'Reward Leader', and 'Justice Leader'. Thanking the teacher for the lesson, volunteering to lead an aspect of the lesson with which they feel comfortable, these would be acknowledged by the reward leaders.

You might develop interpersonal phrases slightly outside of the students' comfort zone. We called these: 'praise phrases':

- *'I think you did well when you…'*
- *'The class appreciates you for…'*
- *'We made progress because you…'*
- *'You made us feel important because you…'*
- *'You discovered a new way to help others learn better because…'*

Clearly and centrally, students need to be taught these positive registers. They, too often, do not belong in their classroom or domestic discourses.

We have known some staff reserve tangible rewards (iTunes vouchers, phone card vouchers and so on) for especially positive language use. Surprisingly, often there are local businesses willing to sponsor such rewards. This is particularly the case when such generosity is accompanied by local press coverage. We were somewhat daunted at the outset by trying to find effective community partners whom might act as role models. But is was surprisingly easy. There are so many entrepreneurs and social activists who are pleased to be given a ten-minute platform. These colleagues will readily endorse your emphasis on basic literacy accuracy and perhaps offer texts, visits and testimonies that help students see the relevance of high quality literacy.

What the students say

It seemed a bit odd being a rewards leader. But after a while I liked the feeling of power! I could discuss with my other leaders what we liked and who should be rewarded. We had the 'praise phrase' cards the teacher had given us and we would use them or things like them.

Julie, aged 14

What the staff say

Honestly, it really made a difference, having students lead the mid- and end-lesson plenaries. They were so curious and actually began to look forward to coming to class to see if they got a literacy leader card. Incredibly, some complained that they hadn't had one for a few weeks. And that's when I knew it was working. When the students wanted to take on speaking roles, I knew things were improving. Of course, it took time to teach them what kinds of things to say if they were lucky enough to get an 'LL' card. But that's part of the job, to help them speak new 'praise phrases'. They began to reflect on their learning in new ways. Now it wasn't up to my teaching assistant or me to say what we thought had been effective progress. The students were helping. Of course, they didn't always get it right. But that gave us an opportunity to talk about what "progress" meant.

Suzanne, teacher, Nicholas Chamberlaine School

Strategy 23 Inventing literacy: help students become inventors of language

Literacy Outcomes

- Student confidence with their power over language.
- A sense that language is a social construct.
- The pleasure of innovation; a sense that students feel they can create whatever word they want.

Getting started

We found using images from a site like www.worth1000.com encouraged 'word invention'. It even helps to let students know that it is thought Shakespeare invented around 1,700 words in the English Language. ['Words Shakespeare Invented: List of Words Shakespeare Invented', www.nosweatshakespeare.com.] Have them guess first and it doesn't matter if they think it's more or less than 1,000. Those who think it is fewer will be surprised and encouraged; those who think it is more can be celebrated for optimism.

If you present an image of, say, a holographic computer, or an image of one of Jupiter's moons, first ask students whether they think it actually exists. Some will say it does and you can introduce to them the capacity to believe anything is possible. We tell the students that before invention comes imagination.

Putting it into practice

Ask students questions about your chosen image. For example, if you have selected an image of the holographic computer, you could ask:

- What would the word be for the holographic key stroke?
- How would you design the screen?
- What would the wireless connection be called?

Encourage the students to invent imaginative words and phrases.

If you have selected the image of one of Jupiter's moons, the questions might include:

- What might be under the ice of Europa or Ganymede?
- What might be the name of the creatures that live there?

Encourage the students to invent words to do with the imaginary creatures, for example, the foods the creatures might eat. Ask if the creatures have a language and, if so, what it would be like. Then ask what senses they might use with which to communicate and whether there are senses we don't know about, for instance, telepathy, or perhaps the ability to travel in time. Who can say?

Taking it further

- Invite the students to follow this up with their ICT teachers. Give the staff notice that this may happen.
- Encourage the students to invent codes between partners for messages.
- The key for extension is to encourage imaginative invention. You want to encourage the ability to wonder. Sites such as The European Space Agency's (www.esa.int/esa) allow students to see what is being planned over the next ten to 20 years. By the time our students are in their mid-20s, the ESA will have launched its exploratory, unmanned spacecraft to Jupiter's most intriguing moons.

What the students say

I didn't know that you could invent words. I thought there was some sort of law. But you can and I didn't know that Shakespeare did. So I invented the word "holostroke" for what you would do on a holographic keyboard and no one had thought of it. It made me feel like a word inventor.

Corin, aged 14

We thought it was a bit random being asked to invent power tools that didn't exist. But I liked trying to make the strangest word I could. The teacher said,

"Which do you think came first, the iPod or the word "iPod?". I thought that was easy: you'd have to make the thing before you came up with a word for it. But then we argued a bit and some of us thought it might be possible that you could imagine, draw and name some technology before you made prototypes.

Terry, aged 15

What the staff say

I enjoyed asking the students to imagine what tools might be needed to, say, carve a face in granite or diamond. They came up with words like; 'Grungikle' or 'Sheercarver' and my favourite, 'Gigablaster'.

Then we asked them what these instruments might look like. We wanted them to think about their inventions' key features, power sources, risks and qualifications needed to use them. What was important was to let the students play with language.

We even managed to talk about which came first, the word or the power tool? It was a fascinating discussion and they were fairly evenly divided. Some thought you couldn't possibly build something until you had defined and named it. Others thought the name would naturally come to the inventor when she or he had done the making. Either way, we got the students to think about the connection between language and invention and thought.

Brian, technology teacher

Strategy 24 A range of ideas to to improve excellence in reading

Literacy Outcomes

- A move towards whole-school commitment to literacy and reading.
- Agreed strategies put in place and maintained throughout the year.
- Higher student enjoyment of reading.

Getting started

A school that puts reading at the centre of its development plan must make a serious commitment to a range of strategies such as we outline below. Often your job as literacy leader is to convince senior leadership that a genuine, sustained, constant commitment to the joy and improvement of reading is central to the school's mission.

Attritional, frequent, courteous requests to address senior leadership teams and governing bodies are, therefore, essential to ensure the leadership's backing for a serious range of strategies. In addition, the allegiance and co-leadership of students is important.

The improvement of reading throughout the community cannot be secured unless there are regular and frequent one-to-one reading sessions. Of course, with limited resources, this is not easy. But there are members of the school employee and parental base who can be invited to help. Parents, clerical staff and catering employees can be extraordinarily important.

Certainly, enlisting this community of reading supporters, or as we call them, functional skill tutors, requires careful and inclusive training. We find that these separate sessions of introductory training can attune volunteers to techniques like those listed below.

Encourage focus. Ensure staff and students are reassured that they will be both helped and encouraged and, perhaps, even inspired by the schools' reading community, that is, its students, staff and parents.

Putting it into practice

Build reading improvement plans for each child who arrives at secondary school 'stuck' at an English National Curriculum Level 3 or 4 in reading by age 11 and/ or with a reading age one year or more behind their chronological age. These students should have at least an hour of reading a day with a teaching assistant, safeguarding-checked and trained volunteer, or student reading mentor. Hearing and encouraging students to read once a day, every day, is about as effective as it gets in terms of improvement

Few strategies are more important than one-to-one tutoring in reading. A few suggested techniques for this process are as follows:

Techniques for one-to-one tutoring in reading

- If a student struggles with a word, give them the meaning and pronunciation quickly.
- Applaud students' attempt at sounding out words with which they are unfamiliar. Helping students to feel 'comfortably uncomfortable' with new words and phrases is key. Without this, they will not consider experimenting with new growth of vocabulary.
- Place the content of what is read at the forefront of each reading session.
- Ask if it is all right to share the reading; showing an eagerness to get involved with the read is obviously encouraging. If you make a mistake in your reading, model how you'd get out of it without panic: using context cues, 'chunking down' the word but don't dwell on it. Saying something like: 'Oh it'll probably become clear later on,' shows students that even adults make mistakes and we do; we just don't let it bother us.
- Invite students to choose the reading material they would like to use in the session.
- Encourage students to understand the concept of syllabic breakdown; rather than reading letter sound by sound, chunk the word down into its major phonetic elements rather than its graphemes.
- Encourage students to let you know when they want to choose texts that do not seem to challenge them. After all, do we not all, occasionally, wish to read so-called, 'easy' fictions, newspapers and so on? You can always recover their challenge journey, providing they are being met with regularly and frequently. It will not do, to allow students 'stuck' in their

reading progress, to rely for the necessarily occasional provision from their class teacher. If the class is supported by a teaching assistant, their time is also focused to those students with statements of educational need.

- Invite students to keep a reading journal, in which they write a sentence or two about the content of the reading of the one to one session.

Other ideas for improving reading are:

- At each week's staff briefing, introduce a list of five new words. These could be generic connectives that encourage extended writing. Invite (or insist) that colleagues use these in their teaching; for instance, expect their student literacy leaders to promote these words in their lessons. Of course, focus on other literacy skills if they are your evidence based priorities.

- Ask every member of staff for their favourite books. Get them to think of one sentence beginning with 'This book changed my life because…' Insist that every classroom has the teacher's favourite books listed and illustrated with their covers and review quotes on their classroom doors.

- Plan one day a week, every week, when tutor time is given over to reading for pleasure. We tell everyone that they should have a 'life support system' in their school bag. This is simply a book, fiction or non-fiction.

- Build 'reading for pleasure' into each subject departments' scheme of work.

- Ensure that the more able readers have a reading mentor from your older student community who recommends reading lists.

- Make sure that your school website has a book review section, frequently updated and differentiated by year and ability. This should be on the school homepage and be regularly refreshed.

Taking it further

- Encourage reading aloud in public spaces. There will be brave volunteers, pairs or small groups of students (or even staff), who will occupy a public space in the school and read aloud from a fiction book they enjoy. This should only last two or three minutes. Try to encourage curiosity: the listeners will be intrigued by what is happening. The more you create a culture where literacy is, almost literally, round every corner the more you will create a critical mass where it is 'cool' to read and write.

- Begin each governing body session with a reading session: have the Chair read a poem and invite each member of the governing body to share their current reading. This can be led by students: 'Here's an extract from the book most borrowed from the library this week.' 'I'm going to read from someone's favourite book. That person is in this room. Can you guess who?' The key is to keep the literacy event short and to make the participants curious.

What the students say

At first it was strange to be told that, because we had worked so hard, we could have extra lessons in reading and writing. But once it started, me and my friend found our reading and writing got better. I felt more confident each time. I knew they wouldn't last for ever, so that made it OK. Other teachers noticed too that I was reading questions better in tests and even volunteering to read out loud in class.

Tony, aged 13

What the staff say

I found it important to give something back to the school. I was offered the opportunity of quality training and there was a definite improvement in the reading and writing of the students. I worked with two students for six sessions of fifteen minutes, three times a year. I could fit this in with dropping my child off at the school.

Julia, parent volunteer

I am a science teacher and, as it happens, I'm really into Isaac Asimov, so when I was given laminated copies of my top three recommendations, it made the students curious to see them on my classroom door. I got so into it, that I would read some of his work, especially when it came to making students wonder about astronomy. Some students then asked if they could read more.

George, science teacher

Strategy 25 How to support students with spelling weaknesses

Literacy Outcomes

- Students with the greatest literacy need in terms of spelling are identified and supported.
- Staff across the curriculum are made aware of particular spelling issues.

Getting started

The specific diagnosis of spelling and literacy issues, for example dyslexia, and the organising of appropriate support will normally fall to your special needs coordinator (SENCO) and their team. They will be able to keep you up-to-date with guidance and best practice in working with students with specific needs. From a cross-curricular literacy point of view, our aim has to be to ensure that:

- Students with spelling weaknesses are identified.
- Support is provided, with monitoring of progress.
- The effectiveness of our provision is evaluated.
- Staff have realistic expectations of individual students, at the same time maintaining high expectations of accuracy and completion – as these are appropriate to the students.

Putting it into practice

If at all possible, try and make sure you receive detailed information on the students who transfer to you from their primary school and ensure that a detailed discussion takes place between your SENCO and staff at the primary school for each student with specific learning needs.

It is quite probable that you will not get any specific information on literacy, for example, reading or spelling ages. As a screening activity, therefore, you should carry out a simple spelling test, in class, early on in the September term. We carried out Cognitive Ability Testing (CAT tests) during our transfer process, when students visit us for four days so that data is available at the start of term. (Carry out the Vernon spelling test, which is quick and provides information that you may miss if students do not have other sources of data.)

Students who score below the spelling age of ten should be tested for their reading age, and then placed on an appropriate programme: these include one-to-one or small group reading and spelling activities. We used one or two commercial schemes for systematically addressing spelling weaknesses, and learning high-frequency words.

From a cross-curricular point of view, it is important that this information is fedback to all staff: they need to know the names of students who are receiving this level of intervention and be aware of realistic expectations and targets for spelling. These should be referred to in the whole-school spelling and marking policy, which asks staff to point out only a small number of errors, and focus on those that the student should know, or should learn next.

At the end of the year retest Year 7 students for spelling, and the results can be collated on a spreadsheet – see the example below

Spelling age	Year 7 Sept 2011			Year 7 Sept 2010		
	Sept	June	Change	Sept	June	Change
Spelling age above chronological age	48%	52%	4%	60%	64%	4%
Spelling age below chronological age	50%	46%	–4%	40%	35%	–5%
Spelling age equals chronological age	1%	1%	0%	1%	2%	1%
Spelling age increased by 1 year or more			39%			50%
Spelling age increased less than 1 year			40%			41%
Spelling age remains unchanged			6%			2%
Spelling age reduced			13%			7%
Spelling age reduced by 1 year or more			1%			0%
Spelling age below ten	27%	19%	–8%	17%	11%	–6%

Example spreadsheet of Year 7 students' spelling

Once you have the information on a spreadsheet it is possible to filter and see the names of individual students who fall into each category. You can look at the year-on-year trends. In the example given it was clear that we needed to look at the students whose spelling age reduced, and take appropriate action.

Taking it further

Share the data with tutors: ask them to keep an eye on those students who appear to be falling behind. The tutors can then take a particular interest in their books; parents can be contacted and offered advice on how to support their sons or daughters.

What the staff say

I can clearly remember in my second year of teaching setting a homework of learning a list of spellings. I thought they were reasonable for the Year 7 class. However, as the SENCO pointed out, for the boy with dyslexia the test was always going to be an impossibility and he scored only one out of ten. Since then I have set individualised tests based on the words they need to know next – basically words they have used and got wrong.

English teacher

Links to other strategies

- Strategy 26 'How to produce a spelling and marking policy' on page 103.
- Extra resources 'Example marking policy' on page 105.
- Strategy 27 'How to support spelling across the curriculum by engaging all staff' on page 109.

Strategy 26 How to produce a spelling and marking policy

Literacy Outcomes

- Students receive feedback that is consistent and helpful.
- Students are encouraged to correct their spellings in a systematic manner.

Getting started

Many schools have spelling and marking policies and in many schools these will support literacy. We found that our spelling and marking policy sat on departmental shelves and was not being put into practice regularly and effectively. While it contained many good ideas and expressed a sound educational philosophy, it was not having impact in the classroom. Most importantly, it was not helping raise student achievement in literacy.

As we explained in strategy 8 'Setting up a literacy steering group' (see page 41) we felt that revising our marking and assessment policy was an excellent opportunity for involving students. We deliberately chose not to involve a wide range of staff because we were not looking for divergence: in a previous exercise, collecting information on the way colleagues marked work, we found at least 20 different symbols being used, usually with no explanation. It was no wonder marking was not being effective.

Putting it into practice

Once you have met with students, discussed their experience of marked work, and collected their ideas of what was effective, draw up your marking policy. You may wish to emphasise certain key points:

- Marking and assessment should form part of a dialogue, in which students are expected to do something in response to what the teacher has written.
- All teachers should respond to literacy elements of the work they are marking.

- All work should be marked or assessed by a process of self- or peer-assessment, or by the teacher.

A detailed version of the policy should be circulated to all staff with a time for comment or response. (We found, given a ten-day turnaround, only one member of staff raised a question.) Then take the policy to a governors' committee meeting to be ratified and, once adopted as school policy, circulate a simple one-page summary to all staff.

Taking it further

Once the policy is in place it will be important to ensure that it is being followed: for a way of doing this, please see strategy 50 'How to monitor the implementation of your marking policy' on page 206.

What the staff say

In my subject area we had already adopted some aspects of your marking policy, for example, insisting that students respond to teachers' marking. What we weren't sure about is exactly what to do with spellings, and having one consistent school policy is much more effective.

History teacher

Links to other strategies

- Extra resources: 'Example marking policy' on page 105.
- Strategy 27 'How to support spelling across the curriculum by engaging all staff on page 109.
- Strategy 50 'How to monitor the implementation of your marking policy' on page 206.

Extra resources Example marking policy

Why is marking important?

- Marking students' work plays a central role in raising achievement.

- Effective marking supports effective teaching. It encourages students to make an effort, because they know their work is being taken seriously.

- Effective marking helps establish good behaviour, because students take more care with their work.

- Marking is a key part of the assessment process: teachers can see what their students know, understand and are able to do, and what they need next.

- Marking is also an investment of time. Therefore we need to ensure it is as effective as possible.

The importance of marking for literacy

Ofsted inspectors training in December 2011 were given very clear guidance about the importance of literacy in the government's policy direction, the 2012 teaching standards and the Ofsted framework. They were given the following information:

- Expectations on teachers to promote literacy skills and reinforce the use of standard English may not yet be fully understood by teachers of every subject.

- Some schools, especially secondary schools, may not have fully understood the increased expectation for literacy to be a whole-school responsibility.

- Inspectors should record effective literacy activities routinely in lesson observations as well as missed opportunities or ineffective provision.

- A consistent and rigorous approach to marking and correction helps pupils to reinforce their skills.

How to make marking manageable

If we teach large numbers of students there are a variety of ways we can manage our workload, within our three-week cycle.

- Students can mark their own work or pair mark. This can be easily done when closed questions have straightforward answers. Students can also self- or peer-assess using criteria. Staff can monitor this type of marking, or join in the dialogue.

- Students can present work orally and receive oral feedback, using marking schemes similar to those used in English or drama.

- Tests can be set and marked on the VLE.

- Marking can be selective: some is marked in detail, other pieces are checked to ensure students are committed and presenting appropriately.

Using marking and assessment to support literacy

Before students write

- Every time we ask students to write we should expect them to produce writing as good as or better than that which they produced at primary school.

- We should insist that writing is neat and legible; it should be at least as neat as the work they produced in Year 6.

- Every time we ask students to write we should explain the purpose of the writing, and therefore its conventions.

- We should model the kind of writing we want to see, with examples available on the VLE.

Good practice in the classroom

- When we introduce new words, we should write them up or display them and encourage students to look at them.

- When students are learning new words we should encourage them to look at the whole word, not copy one letter at a time.

Responding to written work

- We should respond first to the content of what has been written; treat the writing as a genuine communication, not as an exercise designed to reveal weaknesses.

- Work should be assessed against criteria with which the students are familiar. National curriculum levels, or examination grades, should be used for substantial pieces of work, and allow reports to be written and grades collected, three times per year.

- Students should receive feedback in some form at least twice a short term, or every three weeks as a minimum.

- We should use the teacher's pen to communicate, correct and explain, not as a punishment.

- In our marking, we should ensure our writing is legible.

- We should be selective in our marking and identify what the student needs to learn next.

- Whenever we mark, we should make sure students do something with our marking. For example, they should answer our questions, or correct mistakes or misunderstandings we highlight.

Supporting spelling, punctuation and grammar

- We should identify a manageable number of errors – no more than five per page. If there are many errors in the piece we might correct every error in the first few lines and ensure these are corrected.

- We should prioritise: key subject vocabulary, sentence punctuation and common errors and confusions: for example, 'were/where', 'there/their', 'could of'.

- Key spelling errors should be identified (using 'sp' in the margin with the error underlined). Students should write the correct spelling once in the margin and once in the back of the book, on a 'spellings' page.

- Students should be encouraged to check and test one another using the list at the back of the book: this allows for personalised, differentiated spelling tests.

- We should involve students and parents in checking the spelling lists and practising spellings.

- We should use only abbreviations that students understand.
- For clarity and simplicity we should use only the following symbols.

Symbols for marking

Ticks for good or correct work; question marks for unclear or muddled work.

'Sp' for a spelling error and the error underlined.

'Np' with // or [in the margin to indicate a new paragraph.

Underlining with a wavy line – areas of weakness (with a comment or question to explain the point).

A cross 'X' can be used for a factually incorrect answer.

A caret (^) can indicate something missed out – with a comment in the margin to clarify.

If we wish to say anything else, use words.

Strategy 27 How to support spelling across the curriculum by engaging all staff

Literacy Outcomes

- All staff see supporting spelling as part of their role and responsibility.
- Students take greater care with spelling, develop good habits of self-correction and take responsibility for improving their spelling.

Getting started

Many secondary school staff lack confidence in tackling spelling and rarely approach it; some approach it in an arbitrary and inconsistent way, for example by asking students to learn and be tested on a randomly selected list of difficult spellings.

To build consistency all staff need to know the principles of the school's approach to spelling and how they can contribute. It is probably best to agree the strategy with your literacy steering group before sharing with the whole staff, to allow time for key individuals to articulate their concerns about spelling.

Putting it into practice

At a staff meeting outline the reasons for having a whole-school approach. Grab your audience's attention: ask them to pronounce the word written down as *ghoti*. Explain that:

- the *gh* is pronounced as in enou*gh*
- the *o* is pronounced as in w*o*men
- the *ti* is pronounced as in sta*ti*on
- So the whole thing is pronounced '*fish*'.

This famous example can apparently be traced back to the 19th century and was alluded to by James Joyce in *Finnegan's Wake*. It memorably makes the point that

English spelling is not regular, logical and consistent. To reinforce the point you can show that it is, in fact, also possible to read it as a silent word:

- *gh* as in thou*gh*
- *o* as in pe*o*ple
- *t* as in balle*t*
- *i* as in bus*i*ness.

You can then ask staff to identify the correct spellings in each list:

- Liason, liaison, liasion
- Procedure, proceedure, precedure
- Advise, advice
- Practise, practice
- Exhilerating, exhilarating, exilerating
- Separate, seperate
- Diahorrea, diahorea, dihorea, diarrhoea, diarrhea
- Complementary, complimentary, complementory.

Tell them the answers and then ask did they get any wrong? How much does it matter if they did? The point you can make is that we all find some words difficult, and need to be realistic and sympathetic when students do.

Ask staff to discuss whether we should set spellings:

- In a mixed-ability group?
- In a setted, ability group?
- The same words for all students?
- Individualised – the words the student gets wrong?

Point out that, whatever they do, they must bear in mind students with special needs who may always get most of them wrong: how are staff differentiating for them?

Mike Torbe's book *Teaching and Learning Spelling* contains much good sense and helpful strategies; you might like to discuss a couple of his ideas:

- Encourage students to see spelling as an interesting problem to be solved, not a sin to be eradicated.
- The teacher's job is not to correct mistakes the pupil has already made, but to help them not to make that mistake next time.

I think we would like to add a word to the second quotation – 'not simply to correct' – because correction is likely to play a part in our policy.

Having now engaged your audience in some of the inconsistencies and indeed emotions related to spelling, make your key points:

- Spelling in English is notoriously inconsistent – but most of the mistakes most students make can be put right. You can show a piece of writing from a GCSE student that has relatively complex words correctly spelled (often these will be subject-specific words, for example, 'equipment' or 'rhythm') and yet make mistakes with 'there' and 'their' or phrases like 'could of'. This type of spelling error suggests that words that have been deliberately learned relatively recently are more secure than those learned many years ago.
- Expectations of accurate spelling are rising, and marks are won and lost at exam level in a wide range of subjects.
- The national mood is moving in favour of greater accuracy in writing; despite the use of correction software accurate, spelling is of increasing symbolic importance.
- Ofsted inspectors expect to see all staff support accurate spelling.
- Whatever we feel about spelling we disadvantage our students if we do not help them become 'good at spelling'.

Next, describe the way students with special needs are identified and supported. It is important to do this so that you show that students with specific needs are not being penalised, and that your school has pre-empted some of their concerns about students with specific weaknesses. Make sure you do have a suitable process in place for screening and identifying spelling difficulties, as outlined in strategy 25 'How to support students with spelling weaknesses' on page 100. Your identification process is likely to include liaison with your partner primaries, and a simple spelling test for all new students. Explain how you use this information – for example, by offering support for individuals or in small groups on a recognised spelling programme. Let your colleagues know who these individuals are so that they can adjust their expectations accordingly.

You can then outline the ways all staff can help, using the techniques given below.

Techniques for creating a classroom that supports high quality spelling

- Teach words in context.
- Whenever new vocabulary is introduced, write or project the word so that students can see it. Point out key features of the word: for example, when introducing 'photosynthesis' show that it is formed from *'photo'* and *'synthesis'*.
- If possible, teach words in groups – words that obey the same spelling rules.
- Teach techniques for learning words – for example, these points from the National Strategy:
  - Break it into sounds (*d-i-a-r-y*)
  - Break it into syllables (*re-mem-ber*)
  - Break it into affixes (*dis + satisfy*)
  - Use a mnemonic (*necessary – one collar, two sleeves*)
  - Refer to word in the same family (*muscle – muscular*)
  - Say it as it sounds (*Wed-nes-day*)
  - Words within words (*Parliament – I AM parliament*)
  - Refer to etymology (*bi + cycle = two + wheels*)
  - Use analogy (*bright, light, night,* etc)
  - Use a key word (*horrible/drinkable* for *-able* & *-ible*)
  - Apply spelling rules (*writing, written*)
  - Learn by sight (*look-cover-write-check*)
- Set a good example in your own writing: make sure your writing is clear (and your spelling is accurate!).
- When you are writing down new words encourage students to look at the whole word and write it down in one go, or at least letter clusters, rather than one letter at a time. Students who spell well do not memorise words letter by letter.
- When showing someone a spelling, write it, get them to look and remember it, then hide it, get them to write it, then check.
- Display key subject-specific terms around the room, possibly with a glossary of terms.

- Have several dictionaries in the room for students to consult. Actively teach them how to use a dictionary – by looking for likely combinations.
- Teach good habits – keeping a spelling list.
- Follow the whole-school marking and spelling policy.

Taking it further

- Share with colleagues the data you have on spelling for current cohorts of students, and tell them how you will track progress.
- Monitor books, observe lessons and look out for good practice in unlikely places. Photograph effective displays and word walls; interview students who have good experiences of developing spelling. Share the results of these enquiries with colleagues at future training sessions.

What the staff say

My approach to spelling has always been a bit haphazard. I couldn't really explain what I corrected and why. I am starting to be a lot more systematic, and I can see the evidence of greater consistency in my tutees' books.

Religious education teacher

Links to other strategies

- Strategy 25 'How to support students with spelling weaknesses' on page 100.
- Strategy 26 'How to produce a spelling and marking policy' on page 103.

Strategy 28 Making a 'SPLASH'

Literacy Outcomes

- A one week, whole-school focus on your literacy project.
- Staff have the opportunity to try out a strategy that week.
- Students experience a high impact week where every department contributes to literacy learning

Getting started

We came up with the acronym SPLASH because, we wanted to create a high impact literacy experience for students. We asked the staff to help us. And a colleague came up with the acronym *Sustained Progress Through Literacy, Asking, Sharing And Helping.*

Putting it into practice

Give staff three weeks' notice of the SPLASH day. Tell them that on that day all of their lessons must include a reference to at least one literacy skill, no matter how small. You can define the focus area or let staff choose for themselves.

If you have an intranet/VLE site where literacy resources are situated, say to staff, 'In SPLASH week, have one of your literacy leaders click into the Litweb or into the shared area Litbox and show their peers some examples of a literacy strategy'. Ask staff to seize every opportunity they can to raise the profile of literacy and the support resources available.

Taking it further

You could offer the list of words that help students progress via the Bloom's Taxonomy. We find this helpful because it gives students the language they need to extend their vocabulary. Some staff taped this list to their desks so they could use and encourage the words. Here's the language we introduced:

Knowledge	list, define, tell, describe, identify, show, label, collect, examine, tabulate, quote, name, who, when, where.
Comprehension	summarise, describe, interpret, contrast, predict, associate, distinguish, estimate, differentiate, discuss, extend.
Application	apply, demonstrate, calculate, complete, illustrate, show, solve, examine, modift, relate, change, classify, experiment, discover.
Analysis	analyse, separate, order, explain, connect, classify, arrange, divide, compare, select, explain, infer.
Synthesis	combine, integrate, modify, rearrange, substitute, plan, create, design, invent, what is it?, compose, formulate, prepare, generalise, rewrite.
Evaluation	assess, decide, rank, grade, test, measure, recommend, convince, select, judge, explain, discriminate, support, conclude, compare.
Innovation	what if, supposing, say, let's say, imagine. picture, envisage, visualise, see in your mind's eye, think of, consider, conceive of, create in your mind.

What the staff say

I loved seeing students help us launch SPLASH week. Because they said it would be valuable, that gave us the impetus to have a go.
So, in graphics, we agreed to promote connectives and higher order thinking language. We chose assessment for learning as the means to do this. We showed examples of students reflecting on their work in self assessment. We showed them the list of Bloom's Taxonomy phrases. We modelled how some of the more unfamiliar words might be used. It didn't take long and there was a real buzz around the school because we knew everyone was trying to make it a success.

Annie, graphics teacher

What the students say

It was nerve-wracking to stand up in front of the whole staff and tell them about SPLASH week but I was in a group so that made it easier. I felt a real sense of achievement when we'd finished.

And staff kept come up to me in the day to say how well I'd done. It was good that we got a chance to tell teachers what helped us. We felt we had a voice and had been listened to.

Paul, aged 14

Strategy 29 How to promote high-quality presentation across the curriculum

Literacy Outcomes

- Commitment to high standards of literacy through high-quality presentation of spelling, grammar and handwriting.
- The involvement of parents and students in setting high standards of literacy.

Getting started

Some staff may need convincing about the importance of high quality handwriting and text layout. The easiest way to do this is by selecting examples of work produced by more able students in which the quality of presentation and particularly handwriting is undermining the quality of work generally. Obvious examples of this are more-able boys in particular, whose handwriting masks poor spelling and punctuation. Share examples of this type of work in staff meetings. You may be able to track underachieving students at GCSE level, whose poor handwriting presentation might have been addressed earlier in their school career. This is powerful evidence of the need to make improvement.

Putting it into practice

- Stress the importance of high-quality presentation at every possible opportunity: to parents, to students, to teachers. This can be done in presentations, assemblies and newsletters.

- Share with staff a policy on presentation: there is an example of what such a policy might look like, on page 119. Use examples of students from your own school to give the presentation impact.

- Insist that all subject teams produce a sheet of expectations for students that makes clear how work should be presented in this subject area. This can include, particularly when used for Year 7 and 8 students, a space for parents to sign to show that they have read the guidance.

- Equally important is a statement giving parents permission to ask their son or daughter to repeat any work parents believe is beneath an acceptable standard. There is an example of such a sheet on page.

- Monitor the quality of presentation during your regular work scrutinises.

- Reward students who find presentation difficult but work hard at it by displaying and sharing before and after photos.

- Have good examples of presentation across the curriculum displayed around the school and on your Litweb and intranet.

- Ensure that you have support available for students with genuine problems: students who have special needs in terms of presentation will need to feel that their efforts are being rewarded. Use the benchmark pieces of writing to communicate appropriate expectations to all staff.

- Make sure you emphasise appropriateness and the conventions of the genre in which students are working: the writing should be fit for purpose and well organised, but notes need not always look like final neat versions.

Taking it further

- Publish examples of high-quality presentations on the school website and share these with parents.

- Use an appropriate reward system to acknowledge effort and creativity.

What the staff say

From [my] experience as a parent I know how my son's awful handwriting was ignored – and he never got it right. I fully support the initiative to focus on what some people think of as an obsolete skill. Like spelling, it is almost becoming a signifier of a good education. For good reasons and bad, we need to support students in this area.

Science teacher and parent

Extra resources Example presentation policy

Why presentation matters

- The students we teach are still developing their literacy skills, of spelling, punctuation and grammar. To do so they need to be able to read their own writing; so do we, in order to help them to improve their literacy skills.

- At present most of their notes are still handwritten: their work needs to be efficiently presented, clear and logical.

- By presentation we mean all aspects – organisation, appropriateness, using the correct ICT conventions.

- A cursive (or joined) style of handwriting is desirable, because spelling is about learning how the visual image – the pattern of letters on the page – accurately represents the sounds we hear, according to the conventions of English. Joining up letters encourages us to think of letter clusters.

- However, many of us write with only some letters joined, and this is acceptable, as long as the writing is legible. (Some argue that we need not join letters that are finished by moving to the left of the page – letters *b, g, j, p, s, y*. See, for example http://quilljar.users.btopenworld.com/rules.html)

- Correct spelling and punctuation demands that we can spot commas, full stops and apostrophes: writing needs to be clear enough and legible enough for these to be clear.

- Computers have not yet killed off handwriting; when exam scripts are electronically scanned students must write clearly enough for their writing to be read on screen.

- Clear presentation is an indication of commitment.

- The 2012 Ofsted framework makes clear the obligation of *all* teachers to support literacy, numeracy and ICT across the curriculum.

- Spelling, punctuation and grammar are for life, not just for English.

What do we mean by 'a high standard'

By high standard we mean that which is appropriate for the task and situation:

- Sometimes a bullet point list or a mind map is required. These should be clearly labelled.

- A vocabulary test could be one-word answers; if it is labelled 'Vocabulary test' we all know its purpose.

- Longer answers must be written in full sentences and where appropriate, paragraphs, appropriately punctuated.

- In drafted work we should expect – indeed encourage – work to be crossed out neatly with one line so we can track changes.

What about using the back of a book for rough work?

- Rough work soon becomes doodling and graffiti, phone numbers and messages to a friend – not what we want in an exercise or work book.

- Students should be prepared to plan, and believe that a reader – including an examiner is interested in their plan. Plans should be linked to the piece of work, so we can see progression.

- The back of an exercise book should be as well organised as the front – and contain the benchmark piece of work in Year 7 and 8. The back is the place for the list of spelling corrections. Homework should be written in the planner – or if longer – why not at the front of the book? Many teams have very well organised exercise books – with different types of writing in the back or front but all clear and well labelled.

How neat do we expect?

This will vary according to the student. Use the benchmark example as your guide. Some students with specific difficulties will have poor handwriting – and it is necessary to support and encourage these students. The benchmark will allow you to make appropriate comments based on realistic expectations.

Two examples of work

The following examples are from one of our most able Year 8 boys, with Key Stage 2 teacher assessment of level 5 in English and average CATs of 119 with a verbal score of 115: potentially an A or A* student.

The first version shows answers to questions, quickly completed; the second version shows the same questions rewritten, in three or four minutes.

The writing (above) is very hard to read, impossible to mark; therefore unacceptable.

In the second example both student and teacher can read the work – and therefore spot the missing punctuation and any errors. This is a minimum standard. When asked about his writing he said, 'We didn't do anything on handwriting after Year 2. We didn't really bother at my school.'

Setting and maintaining high standards

- Where a set of books is best organised and presented it is because the teacher has insisted on high standards from the start and reinforced them. Many colleagues ensure that the first page of their students' book very clearly sets out the expectations of presentation.

- Parents can be enlisted to support the process particularly with homework. They know what their sons or daughters are capable of, and how much care they have taken. Invite parents to insist that work be repeated when it is not good enough, in terms of presentation, length and detail: they may struggle to judge content.

- Encourage students to peer-assess in order to keep on top of presentation.

- Use the benchmark pieces as a guide: Have high expectations!

- The website www.handwritingworksheets.com can produce printable guides.

Supporting students with genuine handwriting difficulties

- Before transfer, ensure that the primary partner passes on any information you need to know about students with particular difficulties.

- The learning support team will support students with identified problems, and check for any others. Neat handwriting is not an end in itself; effective communication skills are. If a student leaves us unable to read their own writing they are not prepared for the world of work or leisure.

Particular issues arising at transfer into Year 7

For many students, particularly students who struggle, transfer can cause problems because of the increased pace of lessons and the variety of teacher expectations.

So often the answer is differentiation. Some students will struggle to copy down one or two sentences – others will finish quickly. Work out what needs to be written by the students, and for the very weakest, what you can print for them and stick in their books. Other students can be expected to write fluently, accurately and at speed.

Decide on the purpose of the writing. Why are they all copying this? Is it just a control mechanism? In a predominantly discussion lesson you may want them to summarise at the end, but your expectations can be differentiated: for some students it could be three paragraphs; for others it could be five key words.

How we can all help?

- Set high standards at the start of the year – keep to them, and by embedding high-quality presentation you will actually be able to read what students are writing, allowing you to focus on the development of higher order skills.

- Tutors and Year team leaders can monitor books and support students who are struggling or slipping. Look out particularly for variation: why are some books so well organised and others not? Use the benchmark pieces as an example.

- Regularly check work, including the files of sixth-form students.

- Offer students sensible advice – which can be as simple as, join up the top of your *o* or *a*, or, 'Make your writing bigger'.

- Always make clear the conventions of the writing you are doing – notes, first draft, report, letter, leaflet, referring to ICT conventions where appropriate.

- We can all make an effort to model neat writing, and there is psychology at play here: I find myself writing more neatly when I am writing in a neat book or marking a neat essay!

Extra resources Example sheet: Encouraging students to commit to high-quality literacy

Here is an example of a document you could copy and give to each student to ensure their commitment to high-quality literacy.

How to improve your literacy and raise your achievement

- Ensure work is presently neatly and appropriately.
- Label each piece of work clearly and underline titles:

Classwork/Homework	Date
Learning objectives:	

- Use full sentences and paragraphs, unless you are writing a list.
- When you are writing, think about your audience – who you are writing for? What is the right way to set out your writing? Look at examples to help you. Use the Litweb when you can.
- Take care with your spelling. Make an effort to learn new words by looking closely at how they are spelled.
- Use 'Look cover write check' to learn spellings.
- Keep a spelling list at the back of your book; regularly learn and test yourself.
- Read through your work and check punctuation and spelling.
- When your work has been marked, read any comments carefully and sign them to show you have read them. Act on advice!

Please sign below to show you have read and understood these points of advice.

Student signature.. Date...............

Extra resources Example note to parents to enlist their support for high-quality literacy

Note to parents

We are very keen that parents feel confident to support their son or daughter. Please discuss work with them and get them to explain what they are doing.

If you feel the quality of the work is significantly below the level they are capable of, by all means ask your son or daughter to repeat the work. Please add a note of explanation for the teacher if this helps.

Please sign below so we know your son or daughter has shared this information with you.

Parent signature.. Date............

Strategy 30 How to support presentation through peer-assessment

> ### Literacy Outcomes
>
>
>
> - Students are reminded of the need for good presentation.
> - Good presentation is rewarded with attention and positive comments.

Getting started

Once you have established a culture in which high-quality presentation is valued, it is important to sustain student interest, commitment and involvement. This strategy was adopted from our MFL team who had used it for a number of years.

Putting it into practice

Ask students to bring in as many school books as they can to a tutor time slot. Tutors should put the students into pairs up and distribute the sheet entitled 'How is your presentation?' on page 128. Ask them to work together to complete the sheet. It is an easy strategy and diminished the chance that students will feel anxious about their writing. It is better done as a starter or plenary.

Tell your class to discuss your findings and decide on ways to improve or sustain presentation. The teacher can then store the sheets in tutor record files.

Taking it further

- Share the results in a simple tally format. This data could be collated and used to set targets for a repeat of the activity.
- Carry out the activity again later in the year; is there any significant change?
- Reward consistently good presentation or significant improvement.

What the staff say

Students thought the assessment activity was very useful and helped them think about the importance of presentation. The students were generally surprised how with a little more care of their work they could improve the presentation of their work by using a ruler, coloured pens, sticking in sheets. Some were going to make this a target for their own personal development. Students realised the importance of neat handwriting, especially for when examiners mark their work.

Year 8 tutor and science teacher

Really useful exercise – the students were enjoying analysing each other's books and 'marking' them – lots of constructive and helpful comments. I think it would be good as a regular activity – once a term, say, so that they can see if there is improvement, decline, etc.

In order to make it as useful as possible I deliberately thought about who the pairs would be first – I made sure all the boys were with girls, and that people with messier presentation were matched with the neatest, and so on.

I got all mine to add on the back of their sheets the subjects where presentation was the best, and the subjects where it was weakest. I thought this was valuable – could be worth adding to the proforma for next time.'

Year 8 tutor and geography teacher.

Extra resources Example sheet: How is your presentation?

Neat, well set out work can massively improve the impact it has on the reader. It enables clear communication and shows high standards and that you have pride in your work. Developing good habits of presentation will ensure you are able to express yourself creatively and imaginatively and eventually use these skills with confidence in real-life situations.

Swap your work with your partner. Your partner is going to honestly evaluate the presentation of your work, and then give you some suggestions for improvement.

	☺	😐	☹	**Comments**
General presentation				
Blue or black ink is used.				
There are neat ruler lines between pieces of work.				
Work is dated and has a title.				
Dates and titles are neatly underlined with a ruler.				
Dates are at the top right, and the title on the next line down in the centre of the page.				
Writing is clear and easy to read.				
There are no blank empty pages.				
Worksheets are neatly stuck in.				
Vocabulary lists are neatly drawn up at the back of the book.				
Text layout				
Extended writing is in paragraphs.				
Sentences begin with a capital letter.				
Punctuation is used correctly.				
I think you should.............				

Strategy 31 How to support reading for pleasure across the curriculum

Literacy Outcomes

- Students are well informed about the importance of reading.
- Reading for pleasure is seen as part of everyday life in school and at home.
- The proportion of students who read regularly increases.

Getting started

Many schools have tremendous experience in promoting reading for pleasure. This is often the responsibility of the English department, the librarian or leader of the resource centre. In order to establish reading across the curriculum it is important to link up different initiatives so that all staff and students can see the value of nurturing the reading habit.

Putting it into practice

Share the importance of reading with students, parents and colleagues. You might want to launch the reading initiative through assemblies, supported with newsletters. In making the case for the value of reading you can refer to speeches and comments made by government ministers. You might also want to refer to the international study that provides evidence showing that, by the age of 16, students who read half an hour per day are, on average, one school year ahead of those who do not.

The most common explanation for not reading given by students and parents is, 'I don't know what to read'. To pre-empt this, have reading lists available. At this initial stage you might want to share lists of the books available in your school library, or use lists available on the internet, for example, of books for children that have won prizes.

Prepare your school policy on reading for pleasure, which you will need to share with colleagues before publishing to parents. The policy should incorporate the following key principles:

- We want to create a culture in which every student is a reader.
- Every student should read regularly, and have a reading book with them in school.
- The school will provide regular opportunities for silent reading.
- The school will monitor progress in reading and celebrate achievement.

Most teachers will support the principles behind encouraging reading for pleasure, but some may lack confidence in their ability to support the process. Within the staff team there will be great variation in attitudes to their own reading, and part of the success of the initiative will depend on how effectively the school establishes habits and activities that enthuse and engage as many students as possible and create simple systems for tracking progress.

Gather a group of students, perhaps your literacy leaders, and ask them to help create resources that will encourage reluctant readers. These can be displayed around the school, on your website or digital learning area, or publicised in newsletters. This is an area where students can be encouraged to be creative and make decisions. Activities they might like to consider are include:

- 'What are you reading?' Staff, students, governors can share reading suggestions on a website, blog or display.
- 'Books that have changed the way I see the world' – teachers, governors and parents can explain in assemblies, in newsletters or on websites.
- Producing lists of 'Books everyone should read by the age of 16 (or 18)'.
- Books in the news: students can research and write short pieces for display or publication about books with topical relevance, anniversaries or connections to forthcoming events.
- Reading lists targeted at particular interests – sports, hobbies, genres.
- Reading lists along the lines of some websites – 'If you like this why not try…?'
- Inviting authors in to speak to groups of students.
- Setting up reading groups or book clubs

The above activities, and other similar strategies, will probably work best if they are part of a varied programme of events that does not get stuck into a routine. Each year the students or literacy steering group can choose a slightly different focus. However, other parts of the programme should be integrated into the regular pattern of the school week. Pastoral leaders, heads of house or Year team leaders can be asked to build reading into their programme and expectations. In its simplest form, all students could be expected to have a reading book with them, and if they have no other work to do they can be expected to read that. This could become habitual at the start of lessons, for example, if a teacher is delayed.

Additionally, you could timetable one or more pastoral sessions per week as reading sessions. If these are to be effective, and not merely time-fillers, it is important that tutors and pastoral leaders put in place systems to monitor the quality of reading: if students simply have the same book in front of them, unread, day after day, the exercise is of little value. These reading sessions during pastoral time can also be used to help provide support for weaker readers: it can be an opportunity to ensure that the weakest readers are listened to. One way to do this is to involve older students in listening to younger students, sharing books and encouraging reading. If older students do this with different groups of students, there must not be stigma attached to reading aloud to someone.

Activities that involve students in sharing their reading, reflecting on what they have read, recommending books to others and reflecting on the development of their reading skills will help encourage appropriate focus.

Taking it further

- Use this whole-school strategy alongside your support programme for weaker readers.
- Involve parents in the programme, and encourage them to support it at home.
- You might like to differentiate your reading strategy: for example, in Key Stage 3 the focus might be on fiction, in Key Stage 4 a balance of fiction and non-fiction, in Key Stage 5 books with ideas linked to their studies, wider reading.

Links to other strategies

- Strategy 20 'How to encourage boys' writing' on page 82.
- Strategy 42 'Involving parents 2: how to help parents lead literacy at home – supporting writing' on page 168.
- Strategy 32 'How to improve reading non-fiction across the curriculum' on page 133.

Strategy 32 How to improve reading non-fiction across the curriculum

Literacy Outcomes

- A consistent approach is adopted by staff to reading in their subject areas.
- Students will build up effective strategies to tackle reading in different contexts.

Getting started

Much of the early work on literacy across the curriculum focused on readability and differentiation. It is important that we do not forget the lessons learned about the demands students face in different contexts; we need to adopt a twin approach – ensuring the reading demands are appropriately challenging, and encouraging the development of skills, attitudes and habits, such as resilience and resourcefulness, that allow students to access texts of increasing difficulty.

In the term 'non-fiction' we include any reading other than reading extended fiction. Many teachers take for granted that students will be able to read information in books, on websites or on PowerPoint. Depending on the intake of your school you may have significant numbers of students who struggle to access the curriculum. You might wish to start by raising staff awareness of any mismatch between their expectations and the students they teach.

Putting it into practice

Gather information on the reading level of the students joining your school. Sources of information include SATs results, information from primary schools and the outcomes of any screening tests of reading you carry out at the point of transfer. Share this information with staff – but make it concrete: for example, if you know you have students with reading ages below seven or eight, or above 14, show staff what text of that reading level looks like. Even more powerfully, video students at either end of the spectrum of reading ability reading aloud and share these with staff. This will make visual the differences that can exist in any one class.

Similarly, collect examples of text students are expected to read (try, for example, handouts in science) and use one of the programmes available as part of many word-processing packages to calculate the reading age of each extract. Again, video some of your weaker students reading these texts and share them with colleagues – a tough but powerful way of making your point.

The next stage is to share strategies for helping students improve their reading skills across the curriculum. As with writing, teachers should see it as their responsibility to teach the skills of reading in their own subject. One of the key ways of doing this is making explicit the conventions of reading and writing that apply in each context. For example, if teachers are using a textbook for the first time, or the first time in a while, they should take the opportunity to encourage higher order reading skills such as skimming and scanning. Ask students to consider each of the following questions on their own and then in pairs:

- How can you tell the topic of a page or two-page spread?
- Where can you find captions?
- What can we do if we come across a word we do not understand?

Effectively, the teacher is modelling how to read the text, and this can be reinforced throughout a student's school career: even at A-level, students can struggle to identify the structure of an encyclopaedia entry, the use of topic sentences and so on.

In discussion with key staff, and possibly your literacy steering group, draw up a policy for the reading of non-fiction across the curriculum. You might like to ask some of the following points:

- How can you ensure in the classroom that every student is a reader?
- When you deal with text in your lessons how do you tackle who reads?
- Have you created a climate in which every student is confident to read aloud?
- What are the keywords, trigger words or command words in non-fiction? Do you encourage students to identify these words, by highlighting them or circling them?
- Are you in the habit of asking the students, 'Where have you seen these words before? What did they mean in that context?'

- Do you encourage students to use the Litweb to see how the same command word means slightly different things in different subject areas?
- How will you use classroom display or subject glossaries to promote reading skills?

Taking it further

- Share the policy with parents, offering them guidance on ways in which they can support their child reading non-fiction.

What the staff say

I set my sixth-form students wider reading and know they had difficulty with it – so we read a newspaper article round the class. I was surprised by how difficult they found this – and I realise now we all need to do more to teach reading skills lower down the school.

Head of religious education

Strategy 33 How to raise achievement in history by focusing on literacy

> ### Literacy Outcomes
>
>
> - A rise in attainment in history.
> - Students develop writing skills that will be of use to them across the curriculum.

Getting started

Most teachers of history will be very familiar with the need to develop literacy skills: traditionally, history has been thought of as a 'writing' subject, and many aspects of historical study, such as analysis of sources, rely on skills which are also developed in the English curriculum. History provides many opportunities to produce extended speech and writing, and for many students, it is in these lessons that they develop and regularly practise writing formal essays. Many of the points suggested below may well be standard practice within your history department: good practice in this area of the curriculum can be extended to support work in other subjects.

Putting it into practice

In discussion with your history colleagues, identify the specific needs and opportunities presented in the history curriculum. These are likely to include how to write extended answers to what teachers often refer to as 'Ten Mark questions', and how to write formal essays. Discuss and collect together advice for colleagues and students, points that may be shared across the curriculum. You might include the following advice given by successful history teachers.

Techniques for writing formal essays

- To help students answer the question, focus on command words: get students into the habit of highlighting the command words in question and collecting a list of those that commonly occur.
- Give students answers and ask them, 'What was the question?'
- After work has been marked, encourage students to rewrite their answers.
- Share simplified versions of examiners' comments.
- Teach simple paragraph structures. PEE, or 'point, evidence, explain' is one very common structure popularised by national literacy strategies. Some teachers see this as limiting, and they have devised alternatives: one used by some history teachers is PBE, 'point, because, example'. Other teachers use PEEL, 'point, evidence, explain, link'.
- When you are analysing structure, ask students to highlight each of the components you have selected, for example PEE or PBE, in different colours. This technique is very effective at pointing out where one component, for example, evidence or analysis, is missing.
- Explicitly teach ways of introducing an essay, which is often difficult for students. In history essays examiners are looking to see that the scope of the question is understood and a line of argument is proposed.
- When working on essay plans, group students together, with an essay leader.
- To support formative assessment and the development of skills over the course, keep a file of best work, with each assignment marked against a generic level scheme: this allows comparison between pieces and a sense of developing skills. On this mark sheet include a space for literacy public comments.

Taking it further

- Encourage students in history lessons to write in a variety of forms and styles, introducing them to ways that support good habits acquired through English teaching in the primary and secondary school.
- Every time students write, ensure the conventions of that piece of writing are made clear, with examples of newspaper stories, diaries, letters – the types of writing that historians commonly request.

- When doing oral activities, such as debates, court cases, hot-seating activities and role-play, the greatest benefits will accrue when students are using similar conventions, with similar expectations, across the curriculum.

- Have resources available on the Litweb so that students can access support material in lessons and on their own. Then consistency and high quality will be much easier to achieve.

- Encourage history teachers to use extracts from poetry and other fiction and non-fiction that go beyond classic historical documents. History classrooms could advertise books with historical links, particularly links to the units of work currently being taught.

- Encourage history and English teachers to work together, for example, to explore the literature of the First World War at the same time this period is covered in history lessons.

What the staff say

Students find it helpful to see and work with exemplar texts from examination boards. They enjoy feeling that they are in role as examiners. It makes them refer to the grade criteria and use it in their assessment of other students' work. They also feel relieved that we show them the conventions of key types of text, like newspaper articles. So often they are asked to write in a genre and they don't know how it's structured.

Steve, History teacher

Strategy 34 How to raise achievement in maths by focusing on literacy 1

Literacy Outcomes

- Maths teachers feel more confident focusing on literacy during their lessons.
- Students understand specialist mathematical vocabulary and can therefore access the maths more quickly.
- Attainment in maths rises.

Getting started

There is a great deal of evidence which shows that for many students weaknesses in literacy, specifically reading, hold back their attainment in maths. Many students will say, when confronted by a maths problem expressed in words, that they don't understand it: once the problem is expressed in numbers or symbols, they know exactly what to do.

Putting it into practice

Working with a maths teacher, draw up a list of key maths words that students are likely to encounter and struggle with. At this stage, aim to keep the list relatively short and focus on words that cause problems, and come up regularly. (If you look at any national curriculum vocabulary lists you will find many terms, more than you need at this stage.) Print the keywords on large pieces of card with definitions on the reverse. Have the cards laminated and use them in the classroom as part of the display that can be moved around.

In lesson plans identify key terms and choose the appropriate category card which can be displayed alongside learning objectives. When doing work on the board or in discussion draw attention to these key terms. Ensure students study the word and write it correctly when they need it. Use this as an opportunity to encourage good spelling habits: look at the whole of the word and aim to write it down as a whole or in letter clusters, rather than letter by letter.

Encourage students to use these keywords. During discussion ask them to select keywords and place them in the correct context on the board. You can also use the keywords as part of the starter or plenary activity, possibly in the form of quiz: from the keyword, ask students to give the definition; alternatively, from the definition, ask students to give and spell the keyword.

Taking it further

- Incorporate the maths vocabulary into the Litweb: you may want to set up specific sections for maths, possibly separating Key Stages 3, 4 and 5.

- Alternatively, you may want to present keywords in maths alongside those of other subjects: by doing this you are encouraging students to see that the same keyword, for example 'explain', can be used in slightly different ways in different subjects.

- Encourage students in maths lessons to describe problems in words, which are then converted into mathematical numbers and symbols. By doing so you are encouraging them to see the application of maths in realistic situations.

- As part of regular homework activities set problems in the form of words. Ensure students analyse these, for example, highlighting keywords that have been discussed in lessons.

- Develop good literacy habits in maths: for example, when presenting a problem or question circle or underline the keywords. When this practice is fully embedded across the school, it will become second nature for students in tests or when they are unsupported.

- Ensure classroom displays draw attention to mathematical vocabulary and use a glossary of key terms in student work books or exercise books.

- Ensure marking of work in maths pays close attention to accurate writing and spelling, particularly in relation to keywords.

What the staff say

Quite often my students will say they don't understand the question. Once we translate it into mathematical symbols they are quite happy, and know what to do. I think we have to spend more time on the language of maths.

Maths teacher

Strategy 35 How to raise achievement in maths by focusing on literacy 2

Literacy Outcomes

- Students can give sharply focused answers to time-limited questions.
- A focus on nouns and verbs in answer responses; less on adjectival words or phrases.

Getting started

Invite yourself to a maths department meeting. To begin with, just listen. We found it more effective to be an observer for the first couple of meetings and try to learn the concerns, priorities and rhetorics of the team. Find out what writing they do. Find out what frustrates them all. Don't offer to solve everything. You are a guide, support and critical friend.

Many teachers of maths are not sure what they can contribute to the whole-school literacy project. We found that there are some significant ways to engage them.

First, there is no doubt that colleagues are determined to do the best for their students. So, most staff are willing to try something for which there is evidence that it works.

Try to adopt the principle of *evidence, ease and effect*. That is, show the evidence that a specific strategy might work; show how easy it is to introduce, by building on the students' literacy leadership and trying to effect a change that matters to our colleagues.

In mathematics, in our experience, colleagues want to improve students' ability to analyse, process, self-assess and evaluate resources designed to help their revision, like MyMaths.

Putting it into practice

Invite all of the maths team to list the three most pressing literacy concerns they have. Ask them to do this on their own first and then share as a team. Usually, the problems identified are around writing succinctly and accurately reading the question in the test/exam. Tell the maths team that there are a range of techniques that maths teachers can use with their students. Suggest the most appropriate from the list below.

Techniques to help maths students with literacy

- Have students practise writing as concisely as they can. Often in examination answers, students have to write economically.
- Ask the students to explain to one another in writing how to complete essential mathematical tasks: transformation, balancing equations, and critique the explanations for unnecessary words.
- Choose a mathematics exam question. Have everyone write an answer and anonymously display or deposit it in a box. You read or ask the students to choose the most effective answer. Often it will be the one that uses fewer words and efficient punctuation such as the semi-colon to list possible reasons for the conclusion they have reached.

Taking it further

- Have students use evaluative phrases in discussions about whether, for example, the school day should be extended. Limit the time allowed to three minutes.

- Use the same exercise as a short piece of writing. This gets students used to writing with concision, especially if the teacher offers a succinct example first. Limit the activity to ten minutes.

- Dominic, aged 15 wrote: 'The "algebra" word scares people – just ask your mum and dad! However, it doesn't need to be a problem. Think about riding a bike: as long as you remember to hang on, you won't fall off. Algebra is like that – remember what you're doing, and you'll be fine. Algebra is all about using letters to represent numbers, then doing stuff with them. This makes life easier – honest!'

- Using the principle of 'Each one teach one', strategy 14 on page 60, you can get effective results by having students create learning resources for each other. When they use a register that connects with their peers' language experience, it can be highly effective.

- Ask students to write explanations for algebra and put them in envelopes, posted round the classroom. What you want to do is provoke a sense of curiosity and fun. Invite students to take the envelopes in pairs and read the explanations, critiquing, if they wish. Ask them to put their comments back in the envelopes and have the authors collect and respond to what they see. Of course, you have to be careful that the comments written are balanced and fair.

- Our experience has been that in the overwhelming majority, what students write to each other is encouraging.

What the students say

It was fun to read what was in the envelopes. There was a sense of it being like a game. I didn't think maths could be fun. But this made it a bit of a laugh. And that's not always the way in maths.

Dominic, aged 15

What the staff say

I simply used the style of writing I use when I was answering exam questions myself. In maths, less is more when you are explaining a process and that's what we got across to the students.

Jan, teacher

Strategy 36 Building a scheme of work into your English curriculum that helps students become leaders of literacy

Literacy Outcomes

- A whole Year group of students is actively engaged in discussing literacy and producing resources to support you Litweb.
- Students have an opportunity to write for a real audience with a genuine purpose.
- Students have the opportunity to work in small groups – possibly as 'companies', with an enterprise element to the simulation.

Getting started

Plan a block of lessons that allows the whole Year group to work on a topic for a series of lessons that begins and ends with a presentation. In advance of the launch circulate to the staff the sequence of lessons and the resources they need.

Putting it into practice

Launch the series of lessons with a simulation of a public meeting. In role as 'commissioning editor', welcome your students to a meeting to discuss a new business idea that you want to launch to prospective writers and designers. Other members of staff can role-play managers of the company, which you can give an imaginary name. One member of staff in role as the managing director can outline the new business strategy. You might say things like: *'For years we have been a successful publisher with an international reputation. We have noticed a gap in the market, a new opportunity. Increasingly, literacy skills are of great importance. You only have to look at what employers say to realise…'* At this point you can quote from the most recent pronouncements about the need to raise the standards of literacy, comments made by bosses and politicians. You might continue: *'We have realised the need to try to improve the literacy skills of young people demands new approaches. We have conducted some market research and looked at what is available at the moment…'* Here you can use some examples of literacy resources you can find on the internet. Choose examples that appear very traditional and possibly unappealing. You can invite your audience to offer their comments. Then say: *'Young people, growing up with a wide range of stimulating electronic equipment demand something a bit more dynamic and original, which is why we are approaching you. We are looking for new authors who can create new ways of teaching and learning literacy skills. Take a look at these examples…'* Here you can show some examples of PowerPoint presentations created by school students. Emphasise that these presentations are by no means perfect but give a taste of what is possible. Then set the task: *'In three weeks' time we want you to attend a follow-up meeting at which we want to see and hear examples of the work you have created.'*

At this point you might want to step out of role and reinforce the point that this may be only a simulation, but raising standards in literacy is a national and school priority, and that students in many schools have done just this exercise with tremendous results. Confirm the deadline for the project and restate the task: *'Working in groups, produce a resource that will teach an aspect of literacy to students of your age. The resource can take any form you like. Be prepared to present your work at the follow-up meeting in three weeks.'*

In the following lessons students can create products and devise a pitch. Within each class encourage peer- and self-assessment; include an editorial process in which products are checked for accuracy and clarity of message. You may need to select two or three groups to share their work in the final session.

The whole-group presentation will be a celebration of the creativity and imagination of your students. It is quite likely you will be surprised and entertained by the ideas they have produced.

Taking it further

- You may want to make the simulation even more real by asking students to form companies, generate a company name and a brand identity and to write a full pitch for the final session.
- Your successful products can become part of your Litweb, and be used as real resources in your school.

Links to other strategies

- Strategy 8 'How to set up a literacy steering group' on page 41. The Steering Group is a group of literacy leaders who want to take their involvement even further and, for example, help write the school's marking policy.
- Strategy 17 'How to design a 'Litweb': an internet resource that staff, students and parents can use' on page 73.

Strategy 37 Teacher in role: using drama to improve writing in science

Literacy Outcomes

- Improved student confidence with science-specific language.
- Increased student confidence in their ability to innovate and experiment with new language.
- Improved staff confidence in terms of their ability to use such techniques as teacher in role.

Getting started

Invite a colleague who is willing to try something new to help you with this activity. Often these will be those who are new to the profession and who are, thus, likely to have high teaching loads. Often, and for good reason, staff will give credence to such colleagues with whom they identify. We found that inviting these allies in the staffroom to help share literacy can be one of the most important factors in disseminating ideas. It also helps if this colleague is well respected and is an opinion former amongst her or his peers for obvious reasons.

How do you get agreement from that colleague? In our experience you need to reassure them that certain conditions will be met:

- It won't involve a lot of extra time.
- It isn't a huge change that is being suggested.
- It doesn't cost anything.
- The period of the project will be short, though not less than half a term.
- It might even be fun.
- The differences that will be achieved are worth the effort.

This last condition is the most important and should be explained by the partner.

Say that you are focusing on only one class and perhaps even a group of students within that class. Follow the principle: 'under-promise and aim to overachieve.'

Ask the teacher who is helping you what content students need but find difficult to retain. It's helpful if you have chosen to focus on an examination class and it also helps if the students are willing to respond positively to something new. There's no point setting anyone up to fail, most of all the students and obviously not you or your partner.

Explain that using the idea of a teacher in a role is a way of getting new vocabulary or concepts introduced so that students are free to experiment with language.

Putting it into practice

Choose relevant keywords according to the subject being studied in the science lesson. Put these words in sealed envelopes. For example, if the class is about photosynthesis, the words chosen might be 'photosynthesis', 'chemical process', 'carbon dioxide', 'organic compounds', 'sugars', 'plants', 'algae', 'bacteria', 'water', 'oxygen', 'chlorophylls', 'chloroplasts' and 'plasma membrane'.

Place these on the tables and tell the class not to open them. What you want is a sense of curiosity. Definitions can be on the back of the word or in another part of the classroom so that a representative from each group searches for the definition, brings it back and explains it to their peers.

You and your colleague explain in something like the following terms: 'We're going to do some drama and it'll last about ten minutes. No one is going to have to show any of their drama to the rest of the group'. It invariably lasts longer so you should plan for this possibility. It is helpful for the class to know they don't have to sustain the drama for long and there's no chance of embarrassment.

Continue with another short explanation, something like: 'You'll know you've been successful if you've used scientific words and phrases that may be unfamiliar to you. It doesn't matter if you get them wrong. You'll have to guess your roles from what I say. The drama begins now'. Then, without a change of voice, place them all in the mantle of the expert and say: 'Thank you all for coming to this conference. We're especially pleased to have so many successful scientists in the same room'.

Try asking a few closed questions to establish the setting, like: 'Professor Smith have you driven far today?', 'Doctor Thomas, is your new book being published today or is it tomorrow?', 'Professor Richards, is that your Aston Martin in the car park? I hope you don't mind my asking?'

Continue the drama by saying, for example: 'So as you know it's very important that children understand how plants produce energy. And we thank you that you have agreed to come here today to work out ways in which we might do this in schools. So, now, in groups could you now open your envelopes and discuss how we might explain the process of synthesis to a class of, say, ten year olds'. By getting them to work in role, you give students licence to experiment with the vocabulary, to play with it. When they address each other as 'doctor' and 'professor,' you'll find they are more willing to heighten the focus of their talk and to speculate, guess and make predictions about the vocabulary and the processes. Sometimes we find it helpful to have a brief process diagram to hand on their tables. We don't refer to them but the students will use them if they need. You'll find that they try not to or use them briefly.

What's happening is that language is being used in a playful, non-threatening way. It doesn't matter if they drop in and out of role. You'll find they ask you questions, so you step out of role to help. It is precisely this moment you're hoping for, when they have the incentive to wonder, guess, ask and seek clarification. This level of engagement in learning is often as valuable as simply being told information.

Stop the drama just at the point when their level of engagement is high. Then, have one representative from each group visit another group and tell them what ideas they came up with.

The ideas can be measured by reference to science grade C and above GCSE descriptors, such as the ability to hypothesise and synthesise.

Taking it further

- As a mid-lesson plenary, your science colleague should offer on the whiteboard two different versions, one right, one wrong, of the photosynthesis process, using the vocabulary they have just used. Still in role, the doctors and professors correct the deliberately faulty diagram on the whiteboard. Again, this encourages informed guesswork, taking a risk element of learning that characterises students making progress. You need to have student slightly outside their comfort zone and being in role is a safe way to try new vocabulary.

- Let the head of department know how the activity went: celebrate the fact that your colleague is willing to try something new.

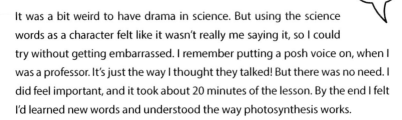

What the students say

It was a bit weird to have drama in science. But using the science words as a character felt like it wasn't really me saying it, so I could try without getting embarrassed. I remember putting a posh voice on, when I was a professor. It's just the way I thought they talked! But there was no need. I did feel important, and it took about 20 minutes of the lesson. By the end I felt I'd learned new words and understood the way photosynthesis works.

Joel, aged 14

What the staff say

I don't see myself as an especially adventurous teacher and I'm pretty sceptical about so-called, 'new initiatives', but because the whole process of teacher and students in a role doesn't take that long it seems somehow to help them learn faster, and when they have to plan to teach something for someone else, that helps too.

I shared what we did with the rest of the science team. Some of them do this sort of thing already, but it was interesting to have the students' comments to show colleagues so they weren't just taking my word for it. I don't use being in role all the time. But sometimes, when I want to start something new, or revise something they've heard a million times before, we'll do it to enliven their interest.

Sue, science teacher

Strategy 38 How to build literacy into PE

Literacy Outcomes

- Students and staff appreciate that there is a literacy dimension in all their subjects.
- Achievement in PE rises.

Getting started

Whenever groups of teachers discuss the need to embed literacy in each subject the example of PE is quoted: how does a PE teacher – who may see less relevance than a history or geography teacher, for example – incorporate literacy into their subject? And why should they?

One easy way of answering this question is to look at examination papers. During a staff training exercise at which we compared the literacy demands of different subjects we found that a GCSE paper asked students to identify and distinguish between items of complex vocabulary, presented out of context – words such as 'anaerobic' and 'physiology'. For many students these would present a challenge to their reading skills.

We can pose the question to PE staff: 'How do you develop the skills needed to answer exam questions or write coursework in Years 7 to 9, to prepare them for examination work?'

We have found that oracy is a key part of practical PE teaching.

Putting it into practice

Encourage PE colleagues to take the vocabulary of the National Curriculum and use it to focus the way they describe, and expect students to describe, what they are doing during practical sessions. For example, they could use terms such as 'outwitting' or 'maximal performance'. Ensure these terms are written into schemes of work and used across the different PE activities so that students can see continuities, for example in different sports. Tell teachers they need to use the specialist vocabulary precisely, with the expectation that students will too.

Incorporating the principles of leadership and active learning, students should be encouraged to lead starter and plenary activities, using appropriate vocabulary. In any feedback and peer-assessment the same expectation should apply. So for example, a group of students playing a mini game of two against one could both describe and demonstrate how they 'outwit' their opponents.

Taking it further

- In PE lessons, as in any other, effective questioning techniques can prompt appropriate use of literacy: the 'hands down' technique, in which the teacher gives thinking time and does not simply accept the first volunteer, encourages wider participation; 'think, pair, share' allows all students time to rehearse their answers before sharing them with the class.

- In some schools, ours included, PE is part of a personal, social and health education faculty. In this context, writing about health and personal development issues is natural: both teachers and students accept that literacy, in terms of reading and writing or extended discussion are natural parts of the learning process. Sharing examples of effective writing in PE and PSHE with students, and with teachers is a good way of highlighting good and bad practice. During a school literacy session in which Year 8 students were being coached by sixth-formers, the head of PE brought us the following example of an extract from A-level coursework, with the comment, 'This is why these literacy sessions are vital.'

An example of poor literacy in A-level coursework in PE

A good aerobic capacity is need because I will face different attacking players each week (some may be fast skilful players which will need me to able to compete with them at a maximal intensity through the game to ensure he doesn't dominate me in the match) the main reason for doing this would be able to execute my skills throughout the game properly. For example making a slide tackle.

Some responses that i found whilst doing training was that after the first few i noticed that i was getting delayed onset muscle sourness a lot after

---

exercise and that my heart rate was a lot higher after exercise at the start rather than a lower heart toward the end 2 weeks of my training.

To evaluate i think that my development plan has had clear set goals in which I have archived through personal reasearch and participating in my training plan I have achieved these goals.

- You might want to present this example to staff or students and ask them to identify the errors, and then ask why a Year 13 student might submit work of this standard, before moving on to ways of addressing such poor literacy.

What the staff say

I am pleased to say we have left the stereotype of PE as a non-academic subject behind. I think we have a lot to offer – because PE is so visual and kinaesthetic we can provide lots of opportunities for students of all abilities to talk. From another point of view, when we get to exams and written work in general, it is often the case that we do have students opting for our subject who are not the strongest in literacy – so actually it is as important for us to concentrate on literacy as any other curriculum subject.

Head of PE

3 The Sustaining Stage

This section include strategies that help you to make literacy a day-to-day necessity. We hope these strategies help you build sustainability so that it becomes normal for your school to keep literacy as a key developmental focus.

Strategy 39 Involving students as leaders of literacy and learning in subjects other than English

Literacy Outcomes

- Improved student leadership.
- Consistent frequent reminder to students of the importance of accurate punctuation and connectives.
- Improved cooperation from non-specialist staff.

Getting started

Use a staff briefing to ask staff to choose two students from each of their teaching groups. These will be the class literacy leaders. Staff will select those students to whom this will be beneficial. They will also choose students whose leadership in lessons may help overall class discipline. The key is to ensure staff feel they can place the leadership of literacy in the hands of literacy leader students.

In reality, staff will only have time to do this with, at best, half their teaching groups. But even this, in an average-size school of, say, 1200 students, could give you about ten per cent of the student body. We found this is more than enough both to train the students effectively and begin to create a critical mass.

If one in ten students are talking with their peers and parents about their new status, you have established that all-important feature of learning: curiosity.

Putting it into practice

Meet the students in an assembly time. You may find it helpful to use three consecutive days to create the energy and impetus required. Reassure the students that their literacy leadership will last six weeks, or any other defined period that works for you. Then they have a break after the six-week process before restarting. Effective learning is more likely when you can build a sense of momentum and remove from students the sense that they are locked into something.

In the three assemblies explain what it means to be a Bronze, Silver and Gold literacy leader. We have included more information about how we defined these three awards in the online resources. In essence though, the core 'entitlements' are as follows.

Core entitlements of literacy leaders

Bronze level:
- Students can help their teacher point the cursor to the teacher's desktop icon that links to cross-curricular resources.
- Students may also take charge of the Literacy Box and, when asked, display the resources the teacher wants, for instance: the laminated connectives grouped into their generic types; or the definitions of punctuation the teacher may want to emphasise; or the definition of when to use a paragraph.

Silver level
- Students can create a resource to be held in the Literacy Box. This needs a simple tutoring session in the second assembly where they are shown an example of a PowerPoint or a vlog or worksheet that has been used effectively in the past. It is also an opportunity for the ICT teaching colleagues to remind students of the array of other sources of presenting information and some key conventions, for instance, 'Use no more than ten words per page'. The 'rule of thumb' for PowerPoint presentations is that there should be no more than three slides. They should involve content and questions and they should provoke, if possible, curiosity.

Gold level
- Students can teach this material either to their own class or another class. If students want to aspire to this level, they must attend three consecutive after-school sessions to learn about teaching and learning through ten-minute starters.

Taking it further

The three sessions focus on the essentials of leading other students. That is:

- Keeping them healthy and safe.
- Thinking about how students learn.
- The nature of the content to be taught.

As with helping parental volunteers to become functional skill tutors (see strategy 45 on page 186) we try to give the Gold level literacy leaders three key 'take-aways' from each session. They are as follows.

Session 1: Keeping them healthy and safe

- Make sure that all the class are listening to you when you are speaking.
- Use the class teacher to help you get class focus. This is a sign of responsibility.
- Try to show as much confidence as you can. Tell yourself that you are highly valued by the school and its community by volunteering to help others learn.

Session 2: Thinking about how students learn

- Students should, safely, be allowed to make mistakes: it's how they will learn and make progress. Students must always, of course, be offered the correct answer to any error.
- Rewards encourage curiosity. So, thank students for their contributions or answers to questions, especially those who have the courage to respond to a fellow student's leadership. Role play what to do if a student asks a difficult question: usually, the answer is to celebrate the courage to ask questions: learning is 'questioning forward'. The role plays support the students when they lead learning in a classroom.
- Curiosity is key. If students can be helped to ask further questions, armed with more knowledge than they had before the lesson, they are making progress.

Session 3: The nature of the content to be taught

- Students look at the evidence from work trawls, via scanned, anonymous writing. They are asked to praise what seems effective writing

- Looking at the same work, students are asked to say how it could be improved.

- Key descriptors of high-quality writing are given to the students, for instance: the use of accurate internal punctuation, the use of connectives and the use of paragraphs.

What the students say

It was brilliant to be able to teach another class. I went to geography, history and science lessons. Each time, the teacher sent an email telling me how my starter was received by the class. It was good to know that the students were interested in what we had to teach and are well behaved. They were definitely curious because it was a student teaching instead of a teacher.

Strategy 40 Making links with the community: how business and social groups can be literacy allies

Literacy Outcomes

- Students see the relevance of their reading and writing.
- Improved progression because there is a connection to real audiences.
- A sense of the learning community beyond the school gates is developed.

Getting started

Dear Parents

We want to improve the way in which all our students read, write, speak and listen. We would welcome your help in any of the following ways:

Do you have a business that may be able to give examples of writing that 'gets things done', e.g.: contracts, proposals, briefs, and so on? We would be delighted to receive copies of any such texts. We need our students to connect the writing, reading, speaking and listening we teach with making a difference in the working world.

Do you work in Further and/or Higher Education? Can you help us with the most impressive, anonymised Personal Statements; examples of essays that have attracted high grades? If you can, could you also tell us what linguistic features you admired or what impressed you?

Whatever you are able to provide we would be most grateful.

Too often the text we use in lessons is somewhat disconnected from our students' immediate employment and/or educational prospects. We would like to include some 'real-life' material for the students to see and work with. So any examples of excellent writing you can provide will be of immeasurable value to us.

We will use them as acknowledged as you wish in our lessons.

Thanks for helping us with our project to improve reading, writing, speaking and listening at our school.

Ask your governing body for information about any business/education/social groups with whom they are associated. Invite parents to do the same. The simple letter on the previous page with the following text can help reveal this group.

Putting it into practice

Create a database of all the community links provided, for example: local businesses, especially those run by ex-students of your school; members of local cultural groups, such a Your Leaders; colleagues from the University sector. Note, in England, for example, Education Business Partnerships offer a useful directory of connections.

You may find it helpful to categorise them as follows:

- Social: for example: churches; publicly funded and volunteer groups.

- Business: any organisation in whose interest, without prejudice, it is to improve the profit motive for helping the literacy standards of the community. An organisation that needs its employees to have high standards of literacy.

- Educational: Further and Higher Education providers in whose interests it is to recruit and retain students from comprehensive backgrounds.

Connect each school subject team to at least one of these community connections. So, for example, the English Department is linked to the local newspaper, the Psycology Department is linked to local Social Services, the Science Department is linked to a local manufacturer of industrial chemicals.

Consider holding a community breakfast meeting to launch the idea of community links, as often employer communities are unable to commit time during the rest of the day. It's better to invite all your community partners to the same event. It's more time efficient and creates a more significant impact. Explain what you believed the win/win benefits to be, namely:

- The freedom for the community partner to use the school's name and logo on its own publicity material. This can have advantages as employers can sometimes find it easier to reach new clients if they are perceived as supportive of education and, more specifically, literacy.

- Further and Higher Education providers often have a commitment to connect with 'hard-to-reach' communities and are thus more open to invitations from schools.

- Employers feel they are helping improve the skill base of future employees.
- Employers are so often motivated by the altruistic sense that they are 'giving back' to the community.

Ask each representative to offer your school one key literacy text that is critical to their organisation. They may offer publicity material, extracts from technical manuals, health and safety documents, trade union commitments to their members. Accept whatever is relevant to your school, and set up a resource bank with this material. Often, students will recognise the groups with whom you have linked, so there is an effective connection to the school.

Taking it further

- Invite community stakeholders into your lessons. Ask them to deliver a ten-minute explanation of what they look for in successful employees and their application forms. This works especially well with older students.
- Try to create a link between the community partner and the school subject department. Arrange one or two meetings a year for all community partners. We find it especially interesting to hold the subject team meeting on the premises of the community partner, be it a primary school or local enterprise. What we find, invariably, are unexpected chance opportunities, like a member of the car design team who is happy to share the written draft of his or her process towards product improvement. It is the unpredictability of these meetings that makes them fruitful. It is impossible to say what might emerge. There are always written texts, explanations, descriptions, reports that colleagues in the community are happy to share that support staff efforts to show how structural and lexical opportunities are not simply invented by teachers.

What the students say

It was brilliant to be shown the car in the car park that the builder owned. He had been to our school and hadn't taken it seriously till he was my age. And there was his car, a Bentley, parked next to another teacher's car. I think our teachers were a bit surprised. We just don't see things like that normally. Anyway, we heard how we could get what we wanted if we concentrated on what really mattered. The builder told us that he won't employ anyone who can't write a report or an explanation or even a way of improving the business.

So I did. I wrote to the headteacher about how we should have longer lunchtimes. He said he would present my writing to the governing body which made me feel good. They didn't agree with me. But at least I tried. And I'll keep on trying.

Jason, aged 14

What the staff say

I didn't know what would come of our community link with the local car factory. But as it happened, the following three key benefits came to us: how to apply precision measurement to profit-driven processes; how to write for real audiences; how to improve the quality of literacy in our school community.

Jenny, Head of science

Strategy 41 Involving parents 1: how to train parents to be volunteer literacy leaders in your school

Literacy Outcomes

- Parents feel more involved in the school.
- Parents gain some insight into the teaching of writing.
- Parents' skills are used to encourage and support students' writing.
- Parents feel more comfortable ad knowledgeable about the literacy content being delivered at school.
- The enhancement of progress of students who are 'stuck' on, for example, level 4 when they are in Year 8.
- Better relationships with the community.

Getting started

Invite parents into school for a 'helping your child succeed' evening; one evening or series of evenings for parents to help their children with writing and reading at home.

Make these as invitational and informal as possible. Offer catering, student leaders and teachers at the door to welcome them. Since many parents are understandably cautious about coming to school, the event needs to have the social feel to it.

Offer some practical tips for encouraging writing. For example: keeping a diary, writing shopping lists, writing 20-word stories, three-minute plays, lists of favourite and not so favourite foods, TV programmes and music.

Invite those parents who are interested to learn about becoming what we call a 'functional skills tutor'. This involves committing to three six-weekly blocks of tutor time working with two students. The three blocks are spread out over January, April and September.

We found these extra sessions work best with Year 8 students. Invite those who you think will most benefit from this sort of regular tuition by supervised volunteers. You could do this in consultation with the English Department. The letter we send home to the students' parents is on the website for you to download, adopt or adapt.

Explain and invite views on the way writing is taught in the early years of secondary school. Offer some exemplars of writing from students in the early years of secondary education. It helps to show writing at differing abilities and in a range of genre. Parents are often pleased and are encouraged by what students can achieve.

Putting it into practice

Show the parents examples of the sort of writing to which students should aspire. There's a virtue in showing writing of higher-, middle- and lower-ability students, anonymously, of course. This gives parents an idea of what progression might be possible. But it is also important to allow parents to feel safe knowing that, when children enjoy writing and reading and make the best effort they can, that's all we can ask.

Describe to the parents ways they can support students if they are willing to come into school as volunteers. Offer the following three training sessions:

- Health and Safety and Safeguarding Children.
- What we know about how children learn.
- What we want children to know about (for example, punctuation).

Throughout these training sessions, the 'rule of three' is key. Make it clear that they will have at least three 'take-away' strategies or new knowledge for each session. Each session should last an hour and the volunteers must attend all three before running a fifteen-minute literacy session and thus becoming a functional skills tutor. In the online resources you will find the PowerPoint slides that we use to manage these sessions.

Session 1: Health and Safety and Safeguarding Children

- Don't ever agree to keep a secret with a child.
- Make sure you are working in sight of a trained teacher.
- If you hear anything that worries you, tell a trained teacher straight away.

Session 2: What we know about how children learn

- The three-part session: introduction, exposition, plenary.

- The importance of reward-based learning.
- The importance of resilience. This one is so important and breaks down into three sub categories:
  - 'Chunking down' the content so that students feel they are never too far from their comfort zone.
  - The importance of 'sticking at it', not giving up too early. We use the line, 'If you're not making mistakes, you're not trying.'
  - 'Keeping it real', that is wherever possible have an actual reader in mind for whom you are writing.

Session 3: What we want children to know about (for example, punctuation)

- Volunteer parents will be working with individuals or pairs of students, so the skills they teach will be very specific. Volunteers may spot weaknesses in spelling and handwriting. It is important to reassure parents that if they can get progression from capital letters/full stops, to commas, to colons and semi-colons by the end of the three six session blocks, they have been remarkably successful.
- Parents need to feel positive about any signs of progress: if by the end of the 18 15 minute sessions, they notice even small improvements: better alignment on the page, the more frequent and accurate use of commas, the time has been effective. Just as want our children to feel success, we have to help our parental volunteers realise that students do not always make dramatic progress and that this is not their fault.

Taking it further

- Encourage parents who are eager to make use of their own resources. Advise them to find out what sorts of interests their tutees have and find texts linked to those interests. They should also draw attention to the kinds of punctuation that you want to encourage.
- Suggest that the volunteers set voluntary homework, or say, for example: 'Next time we meet, I wonder if you can show me in your book where you've used capital letters, colons etc.'

What the students say

At first it was a bit of odd being taught by some else's parent even if they did have the title functional skill tutor. But there was something about the way they worked with us that was different to a teacher, something to do with the tone of their voice and their patience when I made mistakes.

Jason, aged 13

I went with a friend because I knew my writing needed improving. We both got a lot out of it. It was strange at first but after two or three sessions, we got used to it and even looked forward to the classes. We really felt more confident at the end. There was something about being in the library, with someone who wasn't a teacher. Some of my friends were taught by sixth-formers. I had a parent tutor. She couldn't give me a detention or anything. So we got on better.

Tim, a student volunteer

What the staff say

I really enjoyed the training we got to run the sessions. It was enjoyable to give something back. I got so into it that I devised my own teaching materials. We ran these by the staff and they were always helpful. The students seemed more intrigued by what we had made than by what they were usually given. We parents thought this was key to any success we had. It's just a bit different having a parent functional skills tutor work with them. They respond to something out of the ordinary. It was interesting to make resources ourselves. We asked what interests the students had – cars, animals, sport – and then we found articles online that we cleared with the staff and then shared with students. We made sure we emphasised the interest of the content but drew attention to the punctuation and connectives. We were always told by the staff that this was important. Then we tried having the students write a sentence or two about what their hobbies were. Fishing, computers, whatever. As long as we helped them punctuate accurately, it didn't matter what they wrote about. The key is following their interests.

Julia, a parent volunteer

Links to other strategies

- Extra resources 'Activities you could try in a one-to-one literacy tutorial' on page 174.

- Extra resources 'Example letter to parents: Help your child succeed in "Literacy across the curriculum"' on page 180.

Strategy 42 Involving parents 2: how to help parents lead literacy at home – supporting writing

> **Literacy Outcomes**
>
> - Parents are more confident in supporting their child's writing.
> - Students receive consistent messages at home and school.

Getting started

Parents are their son or daughter's first teacher and it is possible they will have been very involved in teaching reading, spelling and, to a lesser extent, writing in the early years of their education. For many parents, involvement dwindles as the child gets older, and the transfer to secondary school can be a crucial point at which engagement seems more difficult. The key messages we need to communicate at this point are that support from parents in literacy is vital; that there are simple things they can do, without being experts; that the school welcomes their involvement.

Putting it into practice

In all you communication to parents repeat the following message, in different forms: 'We want you to support your child's literacy.' This can be re-emphasised throughout the transfer process, but is perhaps best communicated via a parents' evening early in the first term and echoed in any newsletters.

When you address the parents, acknowledge anxieties such as:

- Secondary school can seem more distant from home than primary school.
- Contact with teachers is often less frequent.
- Children often try to keep their parents at a greater distance when they start secondary school.

The following reassurances help parents understand the ways we try to bridge the gap between secondary and primary:

- that students will arrive with different skills and habits, in terms of reading, writing and speaking. We celebrate this diversity;
- that our aim is for them all to make good progress;
- that you are trying to support all of them in getting at least a C-grade at GCSE;
- it is useful to show an example of early writing (with spelling that is not yet standardised, and handwriting that is irregular) and writing at GCSE standard. You can point out that students are on the journey from one to the other;
- remind parents that many of the writing skills developed in primary school will be relatively newly acquired, and without practice may decline;
- reassure parents that the school takes literacy very seriously and you are constantly working on it; and that their support can help children be even more effective.

Once you have covered all of the above, make the specific and direct invitation to parents to become as involved as they wish to be. Suggest that parents are more than welcome to get involved in the assessment of their children's work. They can do this, for example, by making a positive comment about the child's writing at the end of their work: stress that for anything the child does well, even if it's basic spelling, punctuation, and reading, rewards are important. Stress also that, where parents feel their child is struggling, they are more than welcome to frame this as a question to the teacher, for example: 'Could you help more with the "they're/there/their rule"?' Many parents are understandably wary of writing anything in their child's schoolwork. Show them the techniques the school has adopted – the benchmark pieces, the whole-school policies on spelling, marking and presentation. Ensure that in the guidelines and expectations of written work each exercise book contains an invitation to parents to read the work, comment if they wish, and ensure the quality of presentation and detail is appropriate.

Share the school strategies for teaching writing with parents, including the importance of planning and how good spelling is supported. Invite them to check that spellings and grammar errors have been corrected and then learned and it is also useful to show parents how they can use the Litweb to access guidance and resources to help them support literacy at home.

Taking it further

- Find out the amount of support your students receive from their parents by asking them to complete a simple questionnaire, asking questions such as: 'How often does an adult at home look at your written work?'

- You can use the information gathered in a number of ways: simply by feeding it back to parents, along the lines of, 'Most parents do not look at work regularly, but a number do so every night…' Just by sharing this with parents you may encourage them to rethink their approach and become more involved. You may be able to identify students who receive little support and need more in school, possibly from an older student.

- You may even be able to compare the data with attainment or progress data, and say to future cohorts of parents, 'Our small sample shows that where parents regularly support written work, progress is greater than where parents are less involved.' There is scope for an academic study here.

- Share guidance on how to conduct a one-to-one tutorial.

- You might like to offer similar guidance, with different details, to parents of students studying for GCSE.

What the staff say

We have lots of parents saying they are keen to help, but often they are held back; for some of them I think it is the fact that they lack confidence, or feel that school somehow disapproves of them intervening. Sometimes they lack confidence in their abilities to give advice or guidance: we need to keep showing them what they can do, and giving them the permission to get involved.

Head of Year

Links to other strategies

- Strategy 43 'Involving parents 3: how to help parents lead literacy at home – supporting reading' on page 171.

- Extra resources 'Activities you could try in a one-to-one literacy tutorial' on page 174.

Strategy 43 Involving parents 3: how to help parents lead literacy at home – supporting reading

Literacy Outcomes

- Parents are more confident in supporting their child's reading.
- Students read more, more widely and in a more focused way.

Getting started

By the time many children reach secondary school supported reading by parents has dwindled. Ask a class of GCSE students, particularly those who are struggling to achieve at the national target of a C-grade, and most will say they do not read at home. Ask the question at parents' evening and some parents will say, 'We have lots of books at home.' Parents will often want to know what they should be reading. The key to success is informing parents about the types of reading students do at school and how school promotes reading, then inviting them to support the process.

Putting it into practice

From the moment students arrive at school emphasise to parents the importance you place on reading in your school. This can be done in your initial home/school booklets and any web messages, or a presentation at a parents' meeting at which you can make the following points:

- Far from doing away with the need for reading, new media and the internet have increased the amount of material to be read and digested.
- The most successful students will be able to read in many different ways including the following: close and detailed analytical reading in English; reading for understanding of ideas in many curriculum areas; precise reading of questions and tasks in maths; skimming and scanning; researching, including internet searching; reading fiction for pleasure.

In the meeting, parents will often ask: 'What should they be reading?' 'Is any reading better than none at all?' In order to answer these questions and to also generally make sure you are supporting parents and providing them with all the information they will need, cover the following points:

- Explain that reading a complete work of fiction over a sustained period helps develop skills for English: understanding narrative, characterisation, developing vocabulary and syntax, and learning how writers create mood and a setting.

- Show parents how easy it is to access reading lists of contemporary fiction for different age groups: you may have a reading list of books available in your school library or lists of award-winning books such as the *Guardian*'s Children's book award.

- Explain the importance of reading non-fiction: share examples of the reading students have to do for GCSE English (currently this may involve passages of non-fiction texts) and explain that the more students can be exposed to non-fiction, the better. Suggest that parents encourage their children to read non-fiction passages critically by asking questions, for example: 'What is the purpose of this leaflet?' 'What is the audience?' 'How does the language and presentation suit its audience and purpose?'

- Explain how the school identifies and supports those with weaknesses in reading: invite parents to help support this.

- Explain the significance of research skills, particularly use of the internet: how students are taught to search, and how they should filter their search results; show parents the school's policy on promoting reading and research skills, and invite then to support it at home.

- Share the school's policy for promoting reading, which may well include reading during tutor periods.

Taking it further

- Invite parents to provide you with examples of the types of reading activities they need to do for their work, or in their home life. This will help you offer context to students as you explain the importance of literacy. Create a resource from these activities that you can use in assemblies, or in English lessons or tutor periods. This could be called 'Literacy at work'.

What the staff say

Many parents are very liberated when you give them this sort of information; it actually gives them a way to get more involved in their son or daughter's education, and for many this is very liberating.

Year 9 tutor

Links to other strategies

- Strategy 42 'Involving parents 2: how to help parents lead literacy at home – supporting writing' on page 168.

- Extra resources 'Activities you could try in a one-to-one literacy tutorial' on page 174.

Extra resources Activities you could try in a one-to-one literacy tutorial

When deciding what to do in a tutorial, identify the appropriate stage for the student. Look at some examples of written work in different subjects. Are there any identifiable areas of weakness? If the basic skills are not a particular problem, look at the higher level skills towards the end of this list.

Area of weakness	Things you might try
Handwriting is untidy or hard to read.	Look for simple things that might help. Is the pen good enough? Are they applying a sensible amount of pressure? Are they holding it appropriately? Are they rushing?
	Are all letters formed correctly? For example, do letters such as *g* or *y* sit on the line properly?
	Not all students use a cursive or joined-up style, but joining letters does help because it encourages a child to think in terms of letter groups or clusters.
	Practising writing a short passage and getting the handwriting clear and legible will help. If you spot more serious issues refer to the learning support team for guidance.
Simple punctuation is not in place.	Start with capital letters and full stops.
	Does the student know where they should go?
	Ask them to explain what a sentence is. Do they realise that a sentence should make complete sense on its own?
	Ask them to read their work aloud. Can they see where there is a change of subject, requiring a new sentence?
	Ask them to correct missing capitals and full stops, then write out a correct example in full.
	Reinforce good habits of self-correction. Students should use the correct punctuation as they go along.

Area of weakness	Things you might try
There are a number of spelling errors.	Ask the student to read through their work. Are there mistakes they know they have made? Ask them to make the corrections.
	Try to identify why they have made the errors. Are they silly errors that can be avoided easily?
	Are they new words or words they have not yet learned how to spell?
	Show them how to use a dictionary. There are two keys techniques: first, say the word carefully to check they know how it should sound; secondly, look for likely combinations. Students should know that there are different ways of spelling the same sound, e.g. *sir* could be also spelled *cer*, *cir* or *sur*.
	When looking at new words identify the key letter clusters that occur elsewhere, e.g. *ough*. Underline them and show other examples.
	Are there mistakes with more straightforward words?
	Look out for specific issues. Are there spelling rules the student does not know? For example, doubling the final consonant when adding *-ed*. Try to identify the rule and discuss examples.
	Some words do not obey spelling rules and simply have to be learned. High-frequency words should be put in context. Look at mistakes like *where* for *were*. Can the student identify and explain the error?
	When working on spellings it is good practice for the student to write the word in the margin and once in the back of their books. This means they see the word in context, and create their own spelling list.
	Spellings need to be learned, using the 'Look, cover, write, check' method.
	Students need to know what a word looks like. It may help if you work with them to identify parts of the word – prefixes and suffixes – or syllables. Try to get them to look at the word, commit it to memory, not write it letter by letter.

Area of weakness	Things you might try
Writing is not logical or expression is clumsy.	Often students will miss out words or write muddled sentences. Asking them to read their work aloud will help them to find the errors for themselves.
Sentences are incomplete.	Many students write sentences that do not make complete sense on their own: *Walking down the road and feeling happy.* The sentence is incomplete. It lacks a main verb and a subject. You may be able to explain this, with examples. Many students will hear that something is missing when you read it aloud to them, exaggerating the tone of your voice so that it sounds incomplete. Show how to finish the sentence: *Walking down the road and feeling happy, I met my friend.* The difficult point to remember here is that the subordinate clause (*Walking down the road*) and the main clause (*I met a friend*) must have the same subject. Ask *'Who was walking down the road?'*
Commas and full stops are not used correctly.	Look at each sentence very closely. Make sure each sentence has a full stop at the end. Read it aloud.

Speech punctuation is missing or incorrect.	There are several rules to remember. These should be discussed, perhaps by looking at examples in a fiction text.
	
	• Whenever there is a change of speaker start a new paragraph: indent or miss a line.
	
	• There should always be a piece of punctuation before the close of speech marks.
	
	• *He said* is not a sentence; it is linked to the rest a sentence by a comma.
	
	   'Hello,' he said. 'How are you?'
	
	   'Fine,' she replied.
	
	   He looked at her and said, 'Well, you don't look it!'

Areas for improvement	Things you might try

Sentences are unvaried – many are the same length or start in the same way.	These points apply particularly to creative writing.
	
	Ask the student to look at the number of sentences that start in the same way. For example many might start *It*, *He* or *The*. Then ask them to rearrange the sentences or use different vocabulary to make it more interesting.
	
	Ask them to start with adjectives:
	
	    The waves broke on the sand. > White and blue waves broke on the sand.
	
	Ask them to start with a verb ending *-ed*:
	
	    In the corner of the room was a body. > Slumped in the corner of the room was a body.
	
	Ask them to start with a preposition:
	
	    Beneath the shade of the trees, she sat and waited.
	
	Ask them to start with a verb ending *-ing*:
	
	    I opened the door and went into the room. > Opening the door, I went into the room.
	
	Ask them to start with an adverb:
	
	    Carefully opening the door, I went into the room.

There is little variety of sentence structure.	Encourage the student to add extra information to a sentence by using complex sentences. Complex sentences have more than one idea, linked by joining words (connectives or conjunctions) or punctuation.
	
	    I went to school. I was feeling tired. I was also rather scared.
	
	This example has three simple sentences. The following has one, complex sentence.
	
	    Feeling tired, and scared of what I might meet, I went to school.
	
	    Whereas holidaying abroad can be expensive, the weather can be more reliable.

Areas for improvement	Things you might try
	One good way of encouraging a student to use a variety of sentence structures is to set them a challenge and ask them to complete it. For example, write a story or description using the letters of their name at the start of each sentence. This activity usually leads to discussion about what makes a proper sentence.
	Because I was late, I left home in a hurry.
	Every day was the same.
	Not knowing my train was delayed, I rushed to the station.
	Use this activity to show that subordinate clauses can move around in a sentence:
	I left home in a hurry because I was late; when I got to school, I got told off.
	Both sentences are grammatically correct.
There is little variety in punctuation.	Using commas, semi-colons and colons correctly can add extra information and subtly change the meaning of a sentence.
	Colons introduce information – a list or an explanation.
	I left early: I knew no one and I had a heavy day ahead of me.
	Semi-colons link two sentences that would make sense separately, but work together:
	It was raining; we got wet.
	Semi-colons can also separate longer phrases, where more than a comma is needed:
	I have visited many countries: in Europe, France, Germany and Switzerland; in Asia, China, India and Thailand; in the Americas, Mexico, South America and Chile.
	I love travel: seeing new places is exciting; meeting new people, and understanding their culture, is a thrill; I hate home.

Areas for improvement	Things you might try
	In the last example, the passage would read very differently using full stops, but both are grammatically correct.
	I love travel. Seeing new places is exciting. Meeting new people, and understanding their culture, is a thrill. I hate home.
	Using the colons and semi-colons shows that all the other points (seeing new places, meeting people, hating home) explain why the writer loves travel.

Extra resources Example letter to parents: Help your child to succeed in 'Literacy across the curriculum'

There are elements of literacy in all areas of the secondary curriculum, sometimes in surprising places: when we looked at a range of examination papers we found some of the longest and most complex writing in a statistics paper. In order to help students achieve their best, the following year we focused on a wide range of ways of developing literacy skills across subjects.

Helping your child with written work

The ways in which children produce writing can change quite significantly from primary to secondary school.

In the primary classroom work may be drafted over a longer period of time. The same teacher may teach the child literacy, science, history and maths, and the expectations of written work will be consistent.

In the secondary classroom many different teachers will ask a child to write. The teachers will not all be literacy specialists. Written work will be one part of the learning that goes on in that subject, and the teacher may want to cover a range of activities in a short space of time.

Many children adapt very quickly to the changes and enjoy the stimulation of the variety of teachers and lessons. In some cases, the quality of written work can decline:

- Some children find the more rapid pace difficult to adapt to.
- Without a teacher who knows what each student is capable of, in terms of writing, some children are happy to produce work below their best.

Parents have a key role to play here. When work is being completed at home, they must know that their involvement is welcome.

> If you think the work your son or daughter is producing is significantly below their best, by all means ask them to do it again, or in more detail. This is what a teacher, who had known what a child had done in the past, would do. Please simply leave a note for the teacher explaining what you have done.

Sometimes a child will say that their parent is not allowed to help them, or that the teacher only expects a rough or untidy piece of work. Neither point is true. In a classroom a teacher or teaching assistant will try to give as many children as possible as much support as they can. Parents can do a similar thing, with the added benefit of knowing the child so much better.

Ways parents can help

In the GCSE English exam students are advised to spend five minutes planning, 35 minutes writing and five minutes checking. This model works very well at all ages and parents can help, particularly in the planning and checking stages.

Good questions to ask when planning:

- What kind of writing is this? (For example, notes, an evaluation, a description.)
- How should it be set out? (For example, a letter.)
  If it is a longer piece of writing – where is your paragraph plan?
- How do you set out paragraphs? (Indent, or more usually in word-processing, miss a line.)
- When do you start a new paragraph? (Change of subject; in a story, change of time, place or speaker.)
- Who is meant to be reading this? (For example, other students, adults, visitors.)

Good questions to ask when checking:

- Have you presented you work clearly? Are there any changes you should make to improve presentation? (For example, in word-processing, making the font more formal, setting out paragraphs correctly.)
- Have you read it through carefully, aloud if possible, to check for errors in spelling, punctuation and grammar?
- Have you saved the work under an appropriate name, in the right place?
- Have you used the header or footer to show your name, and a file name and location?

Once again, the Litweb on our website can help you find materials

Developments in school this year in cross-curricular literacy: key messages to share with parents via the newsletter, on the website and at Parents' Evenings

- Literacy and ICT are the main areas of focus for all staff this year.
- We are putting an example of Year 6 writing in all exercise books used by Year 7 students.
- We are developing opportunities for literacy support, with students, parents, governors and teachers providing one-to-one tuition. We have produced a booklet to support this work which you may find of use: 'Activities you could try in a one-to-one literacy tutorial'.
- If you are interested in helping support the school by coming in and working with one or two students, one-to-one, please contact the school; further information will follow later in the year.

Strategy 44 Involving governors: using their skills and contacts to help students see that literacy matters

> **Literacy Outcomes**
>
> - Involvement of the whole school community.
> - A real connection between the governing body and classroom learning.
> - A vehicle for helping governors support the whole-school literacy project.

Getting started

Invite members of the governing body to help improve literacy. Use the 'six degrees of separation' principle: invite governors to name role models they may know who can endorse the value of literacy. It may be that a governor has some connection with an individual or corporate body respected by the students who they could contact to get involved, for instance, some major firms and organisations have been known to subsidise schools in the purchasing of e-readers for students.

Putting it into practice

- It can help to approach a few governors first, those whom you know are likely to be sympathetic to the importance of literacy, especially in the workplace.

- Invite them in to join you in a work trawl or learning walk (see strategy 49 on page 201). Ask them to praise and identify those aspects of literacy they think important. You may wish, as we have done, to highlight the high leverage literacy you have already identified through your own monitoring. For us, this was: internal punctuation, connectives and paragraphing.

- Arrange a governor visit for as long as they can manage. You'll need a couple of hours to arrange a pre-briefing and a plenary at the end.

- You may wish to share a few high-quality pieces of cross-curriculum writing. This helps governors compare what they find with that to which you aspire. If you do this, choose writing produced from within your school. Governors will usually encourage students by making reference to that which has been accomplished by their alumni.

- Governors appreciate seeing the assessment criteria against which you are measuring writing and reading quality; showing them exam papers can help them to see the challenges faced by students.

Taking it further

- Invite governors to talk with a class about their own experiences of literacy: some will have found it easy, others less so and it helps students to connect their experiences with those who are in high-status positions.

- Invite governors to offer a piece of text they use in their daily lives. It doesn't matter which genre. The text is bound to contain key language features that have made a difference to whatever organisation it has come from.

- Ask governors to let you have whatever they can sensitively release and something which made a difference to the organisation: a letter requesting a contract, a job advertisement, job description, something that has been important to reader and writer.

What the students say

It was interesting to see an application letter that the governor had written to her primary school asking for a job. We could see how much care she had had to take to get it to look right and be accurate. She told us that often job applications just don't get a second look if it seems like the writer doesn't care. She said that this was because, if they don't mind about getting things right from the start, what would they be like if they had been employed?

Nathan, aged 15

What the staff say

I really liked a number of things: it's good to be able to give
something back; I wished we'd had 'real' people come and talk to
us about how they wrote, and how long it took and how they had to check for
mistakes and so on. I was intrigued by the teacher's technique. She read the
letter I'd written. And whenever it came to a piece of punctuation I'd used, the
whole class had to say, in unison what it's name was. It made me realise how
much I'd used. The teacher did the same later with a few of the pieces the class
had written. I was asked to say which I found most convincing. A tough job.
But then, as the teacher said, that's how it is. She praised everyone's efforts and
pointed out where the children had done well.

Paul, a school governor

Strategy 45 How to use public speaking to improve literacy across the curriculum

Literacy Outcomes

- Students will be more confident in speaking publicly.
- Students will develop skills of logical argument.

Getting started

In many ways, creating a culture of public speaking is to make use of a snowball effect: once you have a core of students who are happy to speak in public, you can create a number of events that will stimulate interest in other students. One of the simplest ways of starting interest is to use the simple form of balloon debates. Balloon debates are small group debates where students are in role as, say: a scientist, a teacher, a doctor and a footballer. They have to decide which of them can stay in the balloon supposing there is only room for three. Start off by inviting a number of students to attend an after-school event; depending on the age group you might wish to choose sixth-form or upper-school students. Simply advertise the event and then wait to see who turns up. Once you have held a number of balloon debates, which can be fairly loosely organised so that students can gain confidence in speaking without having to worry too much about formal conventions, you can start pointing out to students that they are using debating skills.

Putting it into practice

For the second stage, get students to work alongside teachers in pairs in order to build confidence. A good style of debate to use is the Mace style, which provides a structured format. For information on how to run these see: http://issuu.com/esuorg/docs/speech_debate_competition_handbook_web. Having the students work alongside teachers gives them more confidence and initially can be quite a draw for your audience. In our own school, we ran a number of debates on different subjects, which gradually drew audiences of between 50 and 60 sixth-form students.

By this stage you should be developing a group of students with some familiarity with debating conventions who are in a position to participate in external competitions. Most universities have their own debating societies, and many will invite groups of school students to competitions. An internet search of school debating competitions will lead you to a number of organisations, offering opportunities to attend debates.

There may well be curricular or cross-curricular opportunities to build debates into schemes of work. Part of our sixth-form enrichment programme involves a democracy week, during which students find out about aspects of politics and government, and participate in their own hustings. Students from one of our local universities helped support this democracy week, and for them this work in schools provides a valuable piece of evidence to add to their CVs.

Probably in your second or third year, once debating and public speaking are firmly established in the school calendar, you will be in a position to focus on the specific skills required for debating. Here, expert help from experienced debaters, either from within or without the school, will help you focus explicitly on rhetoric. We have found our own students have developed confidence and expertise, partly from seeing other students speaking in debates, partly from the feedback during the judging process, and by taking large numbers to events, rather than have the school represented by a team of two students, you will develop a cohort of experienced public speakers.

Taking it further

- There are many opportunities for weaving formal debates into the curriculum. Increase awareness and confidence across the school by using older students, for example, sixth-formers, to train and support students in Year 8 and Year 11.

- Once staff are confident that there is a fairly high level of understanding of the principles of debating, and therefore that they as subject teachers can pass over some of the responsibility for management of these activities to the students, you will find teachers happy to embed debating in their schemes of work.

- Within the English curriculum students can debate topics that spring from their literary study; within history, geography, personal and social education, science and religious studies, debates about ethical issues, current affairs, resources and historical events are a way of providing a formal structure for discussion. You may find it a good idea to map the opportunities for formal debating across the curriculum, in order to try to build skills and progression. You may wish to use a number of these opportunities to assess oral work as part of the English curriculum. You may even consider drawing up a framework and hierarchy of skills that will allow you to assess the progress of students as they grow in confidence and expertise.

What the students say

At first we were wary of debates. They seemed too complicated. But the more you get used to the structure the easier it gets. The rules makes it better for all to be heard. I found it helped my confidence grow because I was allowed to speak without interruption.'

Sarah, Year 8 student

Links to other strategies

- Strategy 46 'How to trigger phrases to stimulate high-quality oral work' on page 189.

Strategy 46 How to use trigger phrases to stimulate high-quality oral work

Literacy Outcomes

- Across the curriculum, students develop skills that will eventually be assessed as part of a GCSE English course.
- To help students read and understand and discuss difficult texts, in this case, examination criteria.

Getting started

Oral work will be happening across the curriculum: the aim of this resource is to encourage staff to share the skills students need for high-level speaking and listening skills for discussions.

Putting it into practice

Share the examination criteria relating to a challenging grade for the group. When you set up oral activities, share the criteria: emphasise the point that the highest level oral skills involve leading others and drawing them out.

You may choose to give students small cards, possibly different colours, on which are printed extracts from examination criteria of these phrases on. During the discussion activity, every time they use a phrase in discussion they put the card in a pile on the table in front of them. The aim is to 'use up' all their cards.

Set up a discussion activity by splitting the class in two. Pair students up – A and B. Initially all the A students discuss an issue of interest to students: for example, which band is playing the best music; which team is the most skilled in the Premier League; how schooling could be improved for the future. Each A student is observed by a B student, who uses the sheet partly as a checklist to assess their contributions. After they have carried out their discussion the B students describe what they saw. Usually students are very perceptive in what they are able to comment on, and often accurate in grading.

Taking it further

- Produce a poster for display with information about what makes high quality speaking and listening. They can use texts similar to those in the next strategy.

- Video effective discussion work and watch with these sheets to hand. Can students spot examples of the expressions being used? Can they see any extra phrases that could be added?

What the staff say

Students can do very well in discussion once they are familiar with the conventions they need to follow. They can be very effective imitators. Showing them exactly what is required is a very helpful stimulus to high performance.

English teacher

Extra resources Speaking and Listening – Discussion: assessment criteria and trigger phrases

- Speak to communicate clearly and purposefully; structure and sustain talk, adapting it to different situations and audiences; use standard English and a variety of techniques as appropriate.
- Listen and respond to speakers' ideas, perspectives and how they construct and express their meanings.
- Interact with others, shaping meanings through suggestions, comments and questions and drawing ideas together.

	Interacting and responding	Trigger phrases or sentence stems
Band 5 'Sophisticated, impressive'	• Sustain concentrated listening, showing understanding of complex ideas through interrogating what is said. • Shape direction and content of talk, responding with flexibility to develop ideas and challenge assumptions.	If I can summarise… I propose we… The general feeling seems to be… While some of us think… There seem to be a significant difference here… Are we in agreement that…

	Interacting and responding	Trigger phrases or sentence stems
Band 4 'Confident, Assured'	• Challenge, develop and respond to what they hear in thoughtful and considerate ways, seeking clarification through apt questions. • Analyse and reflect on others' ideas to clarify issues and assumptions and develop the discussion. • Identify useful outcomes and help structure discussion through purposeful contributions.	Do you think that… Would another way of looking at it be… Going back to your point about… As you said earlier… Are you suggesting… because… I think you are suggesting because… Building on what was said Can anybody think of ways in which we.. Would it be helpful if we…
Band 3 'Clear, Consistent'	• Listen closely and attentively engaging with what is heard through perceptive responses. • Make significant contributions that move discussions forward. • Engage with others' ideas and feelings, recognising obvious bias or prejudice and referring to precise detail.	That's interesting because… I think another way we could… Perhaps… You're saying that because… You think… You're… When you said…

	Interacting and responding	Trigger phrases or sentence stems
Band 2 'Some' 4–6	• Respond positively to what they hear, including helpful requests for explanation and further detail. • Make specific, relevant contributions to discussion. • Allow others to express ideas or points of view that may differ from their own and respond appropriately.	How would… Why would… What would… How about… Why don't… We could… Yes, but…
Band 1 'Limited' 1-3	• Respond to what they hear, showing some interest, including non-verbal reactions. • Make brief, occasional contributions and general statements in discussion. • Follow central ideas and possibilities in what they hear and raise straightforward questions.	It is because… It's… Well they… Where… When …

Strategy 47 Producing a whole school literacy policy

> ### Literacy Outcomes
>
> - Staff will have key statements of policy available in one place.
> - The process of producing the policy can be a liberating activity, involving a wide range of different staff and students.
> - Completing the policy can mark a significant point in the process of raising standards of literacy.

Getting started

We have deliberately not put this chapter at the start of the book because throughout the process our philosophy has been to start with actually doing something. Policy follows practice. A literacy policy should refer to strategies tried successfully in the school. In the past, some schools have become very bogged down in deliberation about wording of policies, rather than making an impact in the classroom. However, at some point it will be useful to gather together key documents that record your thinking and policies, to share with student teachers new staff, governors and other members of the school community.

Putting it into practice

In framing your literacy policy, you may want to include some of the following sections:

- How to ensure the school acknowledges and builds on prior learning: this section should cover how you work with partner schools or settings to find out what students already know and can do, how you maintain effective liaison, and how you evaluate the success of your transfer process.
- How to ensure you screen effectively for undiagnosed weaknesses in the literacy, particularly in reading.
- How you can assure that all staff support literacy: how you ensure all staff are

kept informed of the aims of the school in terms of literacy, how you ensure staff keep up-to-date, how you share good practice.

- How you map your curriculum opportunities for reading and writing, speaking and listening.

- How you support high-quality teaching and learning of reading and writing, speaking and listening.

- How marking and assessment supports high-quality literacy, including the presentation of work.

- How you monitor the quality of your literacy teaching and evaluate the effectiveness of your provision.

You will find materials relevant to each of these headings in different chapters of this book.

Taking it further

- You may wish to require each team or area of the school to add a section to the whole school literacy policy, which then becomes their own document, in which they show explicitly how their team is supporting the whole-school goals. If this is the case, it is important to check that teams are not subtly undermining the whole-school drive by watering down some of your core values.

What the staff say

Sometimes writing policies can be a long process that has no practical outcome: I must admit, with literacy I can now see how it is so closely linked to everything we do that actually putting the policy together was a positive exercise. We kept remembering things that we have done over the past few years that are relevant.

Humanities teacher

4 Evaluating Impact

This section provides strategies for evaluating the impact of your literacy programme. There are three key ways to evaluate impact:

- Check the students data after two terms of applying strategies. If more than 80% of students are at least making the progress expected of them, you know you are having an impact. What counts as 'expected'? In the UK, it means students are on track to making one level of progress a year.

- Student questionnaires. These are better done very simply. Try asking three questions: did the strategy help you learn a literacy skill; could you teach it to someone else; how do you think your literacy has improved?

- Staff feedback. Try asking: how easy was this to apply in your classroom? How could it be improved? Did you notice, after two terms, improvements in students' literacy?

Strategy 48 How to develop tracking grids to ensure an entitlement to literacy is offered systematically across the curriculum

Literacy Outcomes

- All staff will be reminded of the possible types of writing they could encourage across the curriculum.
- Literacy coordinators will be able to identify and fill gaps.
- Consistency in teaching and assessing will be encouraged and made easier.

Getting started

A grid can be used to identify the types of writing taught in different subject areas: an example of a possible grid is provided in the online resources. There are different ways of completing the grid:

- Subject leaders can refer to their schemes of work and indicate where these types of writing occur.

- Students in a particular year group can map the writing they have produced based on their personal experiences. This is a useful consciousness-raising exercise for the students.

- The grid can be completed on the basis of work scrutinies. This will obviously be the most accurate – but it does take the most time.

Completing this grid in a spreadsheet will allow you to sort and filter the information in different ways.

Putting it into practice

The headings we suggest for *writing* are as follows:

- Year group: this allows you to put all of your data on one sheet and filter for specific Year groups, or to look at the development of a genre over time.

- Task or genre: for example – evaluation, discursive essay, report, diary. Some types of writing may seem not to fall into a particular genre, but when this happens it is an opportunity to discuss the characteristics and conventions that apply.

- Year and term: this allows you to identify when the text type is first introduced – and which members of staff need to explain the conventions that apply.

- Title and subject: these allow easy identification, and sorting will allow you to see the type of writing used in a particular subject.

- Where: to clarify if the writing is done in school or at home.

- Use of ICT: you may wish to identify where conventions of presentation are taught, or what the balance of writing and word-processing is, or whether a variety of ICT packages are being used.

- Examples available: the aim here is that, every time a student writes, he or she should be able to see the form and conventions of the genre – a good model should be available. Ideally these should be located in a virtual learning environment or shared area where the examples can be accessed from home.

- SEN support: what resources are available; many teachers use writing frames, though these should be used carefully. The aim of support is to develop independence by teaching habits and supporting planning in particular.

- Gifted and talented extension: how will staff extend the more able, for example by setting specific targets, offering models for imitation?

- Notes: this column allows you to record any information that may be of use when comparing and developing writing.

The headings we suggest for *reading* are as follows:

- Year group, when and where: these heading are similar to those for writing.

- What kind of text: here we are looking to see that students are introduced to a wide range of text types – fiction, non-fiction, prose and poetry – and activities – close reading and wide reading. Part of the reason for completing this task is to encourage a wider range of reading – why not read poetic as well as factual accounts in science or geography?

- Use of ICT: the availability of the internet has massively increased the range of reading opportunities; how teachers ensure students are taught how to use it effectively is a significant challenge for us.

- What skills are involved – and how are they taught or supported? Completing the grid is the first step towards answering these questions

- SEN support: how will students be encouraged to develop their skills? Differentiated resources may help – but should be used alongside explicit teaching of techniques that develop confidence and independence.

- Gifted and talented extension: this can include opportunities for wider reading, or questions and tasks that test inference, deduction, synthesis, analysis and reflection.

The headings we suggest for *oral work* are as follows:

- Year group, when and where: these heading are similar to those for writing.

- What kind of activity: here you are looking for a range of activities – discussion, presentation, formal debate, role-play. As the grid is completed staff will see the range of activities being provided elsewhere, and perhaps be encouraged to experiment.

- Formal or informal: the prompt will ask staff to consider the level of formality they expect, with the intention of increasing the formality and the complexity of the speech expected of students as they get older.

- Examples available: just as in written work we need to be able to show students models of different types of talk. Videos of discussions, reports or debates taken from the media can provide a stimulus; the resources used by English teachers for moderating oral work at exam level can provide very clear examples of the language they need to use. You can generate your own resources and make them accessible on your Litweb.

- SEN support and gifted and talented extension: checklists of the conventions used in a certain activity can help make explicit to students who find varying their speech style difficult; examples of high-level performance, with criteria for excellence, can stimulate more-able students to develop their skills further.

Taking it further

- Compiling grids takes time; they need to be renewed and revisited. Use them to trigger discussion about the range of speaking and listening opportunities offered across the curriculum, and about how to ensure progression.

- Match your grids to the requirements of the exams your students take in English and in drama, and you may decide to make certain types of activities a specific focus.

What the staff say

Mapping has proved very helpful for us. We have now realised the things we have taken for granted – about what students will have learned in English lessons. But we have also found out ways in which we can help develop writing skills in things like letters, which we use quite a lot.

Head of history

Strategy 49 How to evaluate the quality of literacy teaching: lesson observations and learning walks

Literacy Outcomes

- The school will have a clearer idea of the areas of strength and weakness in the school's provision.
- Staff involved will have a shared understanding of what constitutes good literacy teaching.

Getting started

All schools will have policies for lesson observations and learning walks, derived from Ofsted guidance, developed over the years, linked in various ways to performance management or staff development. The aims of observations for the purposes of developing literacy are specifically aimed at raising awareness and improving practice in a very focused way. At some point in meetings about literacy the question, 'What do we mean by effective literacy teaching?' will arise. You might choose to devise your own criteria or develop one from the example given on page 204.

Putting it into practice

Once you have a range of literacy activities taking place across your school, and therefore will be able to find examples of good practice, discuss with a small group of staff or your literacy steering group the ways in which you can measure progress. Analysis of data and work scrutinies are two clear sources of information – but in order to capture the process we need to talk to students or observe lessons.

You might like to share the Ofsted criteria for observation of the quality of teaching. The criteria in place from January 2012 make the place of cross-curricular literacy (and numeracy) very clear: the criteria for outstanding teaching contains the line: 'Every opportunity is taken to successfully develop crucial skills, including being able to use their literacy and numeracy skills in other subjects.' However, for a specific focus on the teaching of literacy you need more detail and the example that follows has been presented in four levels, in a model that will be familiar to teachers. However, to prevent confusion with Ofsted criteria, and to emphasise the point that these are not official criteria, it is probably better to use slightly different language.

We have identified four different levels:

- Lessons that extend literacy capacity.
- Lessons that support literacy.
- Lessons in which literacy skills are used.
- Lessons in which literacy issues are a barrier to learning.

In lessons that extend literacy capacity you should expect to see school policies in place, and having an effect on language development: these would include school policies on marking, for developing reading and writing skills, for developing speaking and listening. You might see teachers exploring specialist terms and vocabulary, displaying them visually and helping students understand, remember and use them. When using texts you might see teachers reminding students of strategies for processing information, skimming and scanning. When approaching writing you might expect teachers to discuss the conventions of a piece of writing explicitly with students, and emphasising the need for accuracy. The key test of effectiveness will be speaking to the students: can they explain why they are writing in a particular way, or how they approach a difficult text? Can they make links with their work in other subjects?

In lessons that support but do not extend literacy capacity we would expect to see and hear students using language effectively, talking, reading and writing appropriately, taking care with the accuracy and appropriateness of what they say and write. This level of care and commitment should be the normal expectation in lessons in a school where literacy is taken seriously. It will be the consequence of effective staff training, leadership and management.

Taking it further

- Visit a range of lessons using the observation criteria and tabulate your information. Do you find any patterns? Do some teams extend literacy and others not? Can you find key examples of excellence to share with others?

- Pair up staff to do learning walks together with a literacy focus. For example, the head of modern languages with the head of science visit their areas together: what can they find to share and how can they help one another?
- Include a focus on literacy in your standard lesson observation format.

What the staff say

What I like about this grid is that it gives us something specific to say when we are observing lessons. It starts the conversation with our colleagues, and it also allows us to collate the evidence of our observations and measure progress.

Senior teacher

Links to other strategies

- Strategy 44 'Involving governors: using their skills and contacts to help students see that literacy matters' on page 183.
- Extra resources: 'Example table for evaluating the quality of literacy across the curriculum' on page 204 for the full criteria used in lesson observations.

Extra resources Example table for evaluating the quality of literacy across the curriculum

This is a table we created to assess the quality of literacy seen in lessons other than English.

Extending literacy	As a consequence of activities carried out in this lesson, students learn how to read, write and talk more effectively; in the course of developing their knowledge, skills and understanding of the subject they acquire new skills which enable them to access more difficult texts (possibly with complex specialist vocabulary) or to articulate ideas of increasing complexity in speech and on paper/screen.
	• Teachers help students acquire new skills in speaking reading and writing by modelling good use of language.
	• Students learn how to read, speak and write more effectively.
	• Students are encouraged to reflect on their skills in speaking, reading and writing.
	• By the end of the lesson students have developed literacy skills that will help other areas of their learning.
Supporting literacy	Students are encouraged to use language effectively to analyse, synthesise, reflect, in speech and writing, on their learning so that it develops their knowledge, skills and understanding of the subject being taught.
	• Students use texts to find out and develop their knowledge, skills and understanding.
	• Students use talk and writing to record, share and extend their knowledge, skills and understanding of the subject.

Using literacy	Students are not prevented from developing their knowledge, skills and understanding by difficulties in the texts they are presented with, or writing tasks they have to do which are so difficult they cannot engage with the task.
	Students may well be using texts, and practising skills of speaking listening, reading and writing, but they are not developing these skills.
	• Opportunities for developing skills in speech and writing are missed.
	• Speaking, writing and reading activities are undemanding.
	However, learning of the timetabled subject being taught may well be successful.
Lessons in which literacy issues are a barrier to learning	Progress is being frustrated because the literacy demands of the lesson are preventing students from developing knowledge, skills and understanding.
	• Texts are inaccessible, undifferentiated, poorly presented, or inappropriate.
	• Tasks are too open-ended for students to engage properly with the language; demands are too low.
	As a consequence of boredom or frustration, behaviour is poor and learners in general, or particular groups of them, do not make adequate progress, and this is directly linked to aspects of literacy.

Strategy 50 How to monitor the implementation of your marking policy

> ### Literacy Outcomes
>
> - An easy way of monitoring the extent to which the school marking policy is being followed.
> - By collecting data in a measurable format you will be able to set targets, assess progress and identify areas that require further work.

Getting started

Once you have your marking policy in place and you have shared it with all your staff, you will wish to find out whether staff are using the policy. You could set targets, possibly as part of a development plan, or part of a programme of literacy development agreed with your governors. If you do not do so already, then you will need to put in place a system of regularly sampling books, with a specific focus on checking marking. The best way to do this is to select a random sample on a regular basis: for example, request a set of books from one student in each tutor group in a particular Year group or house depending on your pastoral system. To ensure this is a random sample, request, say, the third name on the alphabetical list. Keep a note of the students whose work you have sampled and next time ask for a differently numbered student.

Putting it into practice

In order to make data collection and comparison straightforward you need to record your findings on a simple spreadsheet. Using the marking policy set out in strategy 26 on page 103, construct a spreadsheet to capture a *yes* or *no* judgement with regard to the following points:

- Has the book been marked within three weeks?
- Has the teacher followed literacy guidance? (For example, has the teacher selected a small number of words that the student should be able to spell or needs to learn the spelling of next? Has the teacher asked questions?) By

answering *yes* to this question, you are indicating that scrutinising the book suggests that the teacher has read and understood the literacy policy and is attempting to put it into practice.

- Has the agreed policy and symbols being used for correcting errors? (Here you are looking to see whether consistency is being built by using the small number of shared symbols. Is the teacher writing 'sp' in the margin, asking students to respond by writing the correct spelling once in the margin and once in the back of the book?)
- Has the student responded to the marking? The teacher may well have followed marking policy guidance but not expected students to respond.
- Is there a spelling list in use the back of the book?

The intention is that these are closed questions and that it is possible to record whether or not these points are in place. The aim of the activity here is to monitor implementation: other activities, including lesson observation and more detailed work scrutinies can assess the impact of the marking policy and assessment generally.

The spreadsheet (see online resource: Litbox) should score 1 each time one of the criteria is successfully fulfilled: therefore, if you have a book where all criteria are being met it will score five marks. The spreadsheet can be totalled up in two ways: vertically, down each of the columns will give you a sum total for each of the subjects. At the right-hand side of the table you will see a percentage score for each of the different criteria. So, for example, you could say that 75 per cent of books have been marked within three weeks but in only ten per cent of the books students have responded to the marking. In order to calculate percentages a possible score row and column have been created

Take into account the fact that you may well have missing books. When this occurs, indicate *yes* for the 'No book' option (when completing the spreadsheet that means typing the number 1 into the appropriate cell) and the percentage score will be calculated taking the number of books available into account.

As you will see at the bottom of the table, the following questions are answered automatically:

- What percentage of books have been marked within three weeks?
- What percentage show teachers following guidance?
- What percentage show teachers using the agreed policy and symbols?

- What percentage show evidence of students responding to teachers marking?
- What percentage have a spelling list in use?

Taking it further

- You could ask heads of subject or other team leaders to monitor marking in their teams on a regular basis, using this recording system. In implementing your school marking assessment system, you may set yourself targets for completion and use this monitoring system to assess progress towards these targets.
- Once you have some data on the extent to which your school marking assessment policy is being followed, you may want to assess the impact of the policy: in this case you will need to use some of the evaluation tools described elsewhere in this book.
- Depending on the culture of your school, you may want to introduce a competitive element to the sharing of the results of this monitoring. It is surprising how motivating knowing that you are at the bottom or top of the league table is for colleagues; it will certainly help you identify those individuals or teams where further monetary and support would be advisable.

What the staff say

Some of us finding marking difficult to do consistently and regularly, but it is vital, and all of us focus on things more if we know someone is taking notice of what we are doing. It helps us all – so we need to work together to make it happen.

Head of humanities

Link to other strategies

- Strategy 26 'How to produce a spelling and marking policy' on page 103.

Strategy 51 How to use simple questionnaires to evaluate attitudes to literacy

Literacy Outcomes

- You will have a simple way of measuring changes in student attitudes to the work you're doing.
- You will be able to chart progress and celebrate success.

Getting started

At the start of any project, you may wish to carry out a baseline assessment of attitudes, including confidence in handling any one of the skills that you are helping to improve. We have created very simple questionnaires, which can be used in conjunction with hard statistical evidence of changes in attainment.

Putting it into practice

In order to make tracking easy, choose a limited number of items about which you're going to ask questions. The first example below shows a questionnaire we used to record the changes in attitude brought about by the literacy leaders' activity.

This questionnaire should be intentionally kept simple, and should elicit a range of interesting responses. When we carried out this questionnaire process for the first time with our small group of students who delivered lesson starters, the responses were very positive.

Questionnaire for literacy leaders

- Which project were you involved in? When?
- Which Year group, and member of staff did you work with? What subject did you visit?
- What were the aims of the project?
- What exactly did you do?
- How do you feel the activities went? How successful where they?
- Did anything surprise you?
- Have you any suggestions for the future? How could this project be extended or developed?
- What have you gained from the project?
- Please complete the tick box section.

	Statement	Strongly agree	Agree	Neither agree nor disagree	Disagree	Don't know
1	Before doing the project I was slightly nervous about it.					
2	By doing the project I have gained confidence.					
3	I have learned things about literacy by doing the project.					
4	I think the project has helped others learn.					
5	I would recommend being involved in this project to others.					
6	I would be interested in doing a similar project in future.					

The second example of a questionnaire below was given to students who were to receive one-to-one tuition from sixth-form students or parent volunteers, our functional skills tutors.

Start with simple questions to invite students to begin thinking about school and themselves as learners. Responses to these initial questions will give your tutors a starting point for discussion.

Ask students to complete this questionnaire before they begin the project and again afterwards. In order to find some quantitative measure of progress, assign a numerical value to each of the responses: *strongly agree* scores *5*, *strongly disagree* scores *1*. Consequently, a student who was confident in the areas mentioned in questions 1–10, which are focused on more specific skills, would score 50 overall.

Questionnaire for students receiving one-to-one support

- Which subjects do you most enjoy at school? Why?
- Which subjects do you least enjoy? Why?
- What do you like to do when you are not at school?
- Now please tell us a bit about your work in English. Please choose one option for each statement. Which statement best fits you?

	Statement	Strongly agree	Agree	Neither agree nor disagree	Disagree	Strongly disagree
1	I have lots of ideas for writing.					
2	I write quickly.					
3	I write neatly.					
4	I spell accurately.					
5	I write proper sentences.					
6	I use a range of vocabulary.					
7	I use full stops accurately.					
8	I use commas accurately.					

	Statement	Strongly agree	Agree	Neither agree nor disagree	Disagree	Strongly disagree
9	I use paragraphs accurately.					
10	I use colons and semi-colons accurately.					
11	I enjoy reading.					
12	I enjoy writing.					
13	I am making good progress in English.					

At the end of the one-to-one tuition project carry out a second questionnaire, with questions requiring a free-text response. Then ask students to complete a grid set out as before. Once again, allocate a five-point scale to these questions. By tabulating the results, and subtracting the scores from the first questionnaire from the second, you will come up with a grid, showing progress in attitudes to each of these components. By using conditional formatting you can highlight areas of progress; by summing the differences you can see, where, according to the students' self-perception, we have made the greatest differences. When we first used this questionnaire we found students reporting growing confidence.

Follow-up questionnaire for students receiving one-to-one support

- What have you enjoyed or found helpful in these sessions?
- When we run sessions like this in future, are there ways we can make them even better?

Please answer tick the appropriate boxes in the table below.

	Statement	Strongly agree	Agree	Neither agree nor disagree	Disagree	Strongly disagree
1	I have found that I can stop making small common mistakes.					
2	I have learned how to use colons and make my writing better and longer.					
3	I have enjoyed it and it has helped very much with my punctuation.					
4	I have learned about semi colons and how to use them in sentences.					

Taking it further

- You might wish to triangulate these attitudinal changes with assessment data – perhaps by identifying progress in specific skills, for example, use of punctuation. Work scrutinies can be a good source of information.
- Electronic copies of the grids are available online. These can be customised for your own use.

Strategy 52 How to use simple questionnaires to raise staff expectations

Literacy Outcomes

- Staff will have raised awareness of the knowledge about language students bring to the school.
- As a consequence staff will have increased expectations of what students are capable of.

Getting started

If you have very strong links with a partner primary school, you may be able to share information with your colleagues on ways in which knowledge about language is explicitly taught to your students before they reach your school. If not, the programmes of study for the National Curriculum, the literacy strategy, will give you a good idea of the kinds of things students have been taught at Key Stage 1 and 2 in England, for a number of years. While structure of the curriculum may change, it is likely that some expectations will increase rather than diminish in this area.

Putting it into practice

Draw up a list of literacy terms or ideas and produce a table as over page.

When I learned it	Literacy term or idea	When I think it is introduced in school	When should it be introduced – according to the national strategy?
	Adjective		
	Semi-colon		
	Rhetorical question		
	Preposition		
	Metaphor		
	First, second, third person		
	Thesaurus		
	Bibliography		
	Conjunction		
	Imperative verb		
	Voice: active, passive		
	Complex sentence		

Issue this list to colleagues, possibly as part of a training session; we found it useful during the starter activity to put on the table in order to stimulate discussion. Later in the session, when you have talked about raising expectations, and sharing teaching of literacy skills by using terms explicitly, ask colleagues to share their thoughts. It is highly likely that many secondary teachers will explain that they are not confident about a number of these terms, that they were not taught them explicitly at school, or that they did learn them but only when studying foreign language. At this point reveal the answers:

When I learned it	Literacy term or idea	When I think it is introduced in school	When should it be introduced – according to the national strategy?
	Adjective		Year 3
	Semi-colon		Year 4
	Rhetorical question		Year 5
	Preposition		Year 5
	Metaphor		Year 5
	First, second, third person		Year 3
	Thesaurus		Year3
	Bibliography		Year 3
	Conjunction		Year 3
	Imperative verb		Year 5
	Voice: active, passive		Year 6
	Complex sentence		Year 6

It is likely that staff will be surprised: the point you can make is that, while some students will have not grasped these terms, some will, and we are not building on prior learning if we do not take account of this.

This activity works well alongside other tasks which involve looking at the quality of work students can complete at primary school.

Taking it further

The following example of an additional questionnaire arose as a result of a visit to a Year 6 literacy class. We wanted to know even more about the students prior knowledge and then share that information with staff. The pupils seemed very familiar with terms used to describe language; in order to find some way of measuring this, the students were given the questionnaire below. The questionnaire gives an indication of their confidence in knowing the names for these concepts, rather than testing their understanding, but it is easy to collate.

In order to tabulate results it is possible to count the number of times a student claims to know the term; or we can allocate a score of two for *'I know what this word or phrase means'*, and one for *'I have heard this but I am not sure what it means'*. Both give a numerical total, and the results can be tabulated on a grid for a whole group of students, which will also indicate which words are most and least familiar for the group as a whole.

We first carried out this questionnaire with the Year 6 class being observed in a primary school, then with a Year 7 mixed class, and finally a Year 8 tutor group. What was most striking was that the results were remarkably similar for each group. This might indicate that students had retained what they knew from primary school, but on average had not learned more.

One of the ways we used this evidence was to point out to staff what students arriving in Year 6 already knew, and challenge them to deepen and extend their thinking.

		I know what this word or phrase means	I have heard this but I am not sure what it means	I do not know this word or phrase
Names of types of words:				
1	Verb			
2	Noun			
3	Adjective			
4	Adverb			
5	Pronoun			
6	Preposition			
7	Conjunction			
8	Interjection			
9	Singular			
10	Plural			
	Total			

		I know what this word or phrase means	I have heard this but I am not sure what it means	I do not know this word or phrase
Words to help us describe sentences:				
11	Sentence			
12	Clause			
13	Main clause			
14	Subordinate clause			
15	Embedded clause			
16	Active			
17	Passive			
18	Imperative			
19	Phrase			
20	Statement			
	Total			
Words to help us to describe punctuation:				
21	Full-stop			
22	Comma			
23	Speech marks			
24	Apostrophe			
25	Semi-colon			
26	Colon			
27	Ellipsis			
28	Dashes			
29	Brackets			
30	Hyphen			
	Total			

		I know what this word or phrase means	I have heard this but I am not sure what it means	I do not know this word or phrase
Words to help us describe styles of writing:				
31	Persuasive			
32	Informative			
33	Argumentative			
34	Formal			
35	Informal			
36	Standard English			
37	Dialect			
38	Rhetorical questions			
39	Rule of three			
40	Narrative			
	Total			
	Overall totals:			

What the staff say

I must admit, the results of these questionnaires came as a surprise to me, and it shows that we have a lot of work to do to build on what students already know. Just because we did not learn these words in school we assume that students coming to us will not have done so. Once this was made aware to me I started using this terminology, and I am pleased to say that the students were able to recall much of it.

English teacher

5 Working with Others

When you are ready, we hope you'll feel encouraged to share and build your literacy project with key partners in your local and wider context.

Strategy 53 How to use the web to connect your school to others and have students designing literacy materials online

Literacy Outcomes

- A motivating sense for students that they are producing material for a real audience.
- The involvement of parents and the wider community including local partner schools.
- Instant access to literacy learning materials on a wide range of hardware from PC to tablet form.

Getting started

Invite students to create a website with the literacy resources they have made, telling them that it will be internationally available. Obtain a web domain will be easily remembered. We went for 'Chenderit Litweb' (shortly, incidentally, to be followed by the 'Chenderit Mathweb'. This is a similar website with open access to student-teacher co-created materials focusing on numeracy). The site can be found at www.chenderit/litweb/info

Putting it into practice

Provide the students with a brief so that they understand that, after logging on, a visitor to the site should be able to get to a literacy help resource in three clicks or less. Our brief was:

- Design a simple website that had a clear, uncluttered look.
- Focus on writing, reading and speaking and listening.
- Make it accessible for students and their parents.
- Within three clicks, the reader should be able to access support material.

Also tell the students that the homepage site should contain everything a visitor would need in one screen view and that the presentation should be very simple. Then ask students to upload materials, vetted by staff. This can be quite a big task so it's helpful to have a team of 'allies' who will help. You should only need about ten staff willing to edit and quality assure the content. In most schools, this is achievable, spread between qualified teachers and teaching assistant colleagues. Also ask older students to take the lead in editing and quality assuring the work produced by their younger peers. This is all part of the literacy community project. The more you show checking for accuracy the better. You will find students are motivated to edit by the idea of launching the resource onto the internet.

In an average-sized school of 1100, about 110 students will submit learning materials. This is self-evidently significant. It is also significant to have members of staff asking students to come to their lessons and lead a ten-minute starter on, say, connectives. Surely, we want our schools to be co-constructive learning environments. We, as educators, take the lead. And we show our students how they can share in this. Students can be effective educators. The old adage that you really learn something when you have to teach it, is true.

Taking it further

Ask students to create an application, or 'app', for a mobile phone. Encourage students to find the technology to create the app. Ask students to create it and let students know about it through assemblies. Clicking on the app should take you to the Litweb and its resources and create a curiosity about literacy: it is so important to have a 'cool' intriguing resonance around literacy.

This can be as an enterprise commission to a group recommended by your colleagues. This is quicker, but less like the business process. You could invite designs and offer iTunes or phone vouchers as a reward.

What the students say

It is good to know that we would be making things that could be useful where English language was being taught. We never know who has used it because we don't invite a feedback process for safety reasons. And we don't put our names on our internet-available work also. But it's still rewarding just to know it's out there.

James, aged 15

What the parents say

We are proud of what our children have done. They were so keen to show us what they had made and how to find it on the web. The school's VLE is also good. The advantage of the Litweb is that we don't need a password or log-in and I've got too many of these already. We haven't found any other student-created site about literacy. And we use what the students have uploaded to help our children write essays, especially the material on connectives. We have children taking post-16 exams who find useful PowerPoints made, as it happens, by students that are only 13.

Alice, parent

Strategy 54 How to share good practice beyond your school

Literacy Outcomes

- By sharing your work with others you will generate new ideas and form a clearer sense of what you are doing.
- Involving students as ambassadors helps develop their literacy skills as well as motivate them to be leaders in literacy within your own community.
- Students are encouraged to take the lead in building literacy into the DNA of your school.
- The creation of a students' literacy steering group in your school.
- The commitment of your school to a literacy conference once or bi-annually.
- Your students know that they are obligated to their participation in improving literacy, both in your school, and that of others.
- An enhancement of the culture in your school that literacy has a significance. An improvement to the quality of cross-curricular literacy by encouraging students to ask their teachers how they can get involved in the enhancement of literacy in your school.

Getting started

For us, presenting ideas to an audience has always been within our literacy journey. Because we had tried some of our literacy techniques in other schools, and started off with small practical examples, in this case the older students working as literacy tutors with younger students, and our literacy leaders, we had a small group of students who were keen to share their experiences. This part of our work to create a literacy community involved getting those students to explain to others what they had done.

Putting it into practice

Create a 'Google group' of like-minded colleagues. Make it clear that it will be temporary, secure and only exist for as long as members find it useful. It is exceptionally easy to set up via www.google.co.uk. We found the key was to make it clear this would be expedient and transitory. One of the many virtues of web-based links is their temporary longevity. Setting up an e-group with the intention it lasts for many years, is setting yourself and your participants up for disappointment. Build up a network of supportive schools; regularly visit one another and share your work.

Involve your more senior students in planning events and sustaining communication; you may even build up networks in which students participate or communicate with other students. Devolve responsibility for managing communications, for example, a section of your school website, or a blog to students with particular skills and interests: aim to build a small team that allows for succession planning and continued development of these activities when key individuals have left school.

Taking it further

- Work with groups such as SSAT and the National Literacy Trust to access their splendid materials and networks. We found them well worth the money.
- Ensure that the school development has literacy at its core.

What the students say

We were shown some facts and figures about literacy in our school. It showed, for instance, that some boys at our school, don't do as well in English as boys in other schools. It's kind of like football: you don't want your team to do worse than others. When we looked at what other students had written I thought: "Well if that's what someone my age can do, then why not me?"

Nathan, Year 10

Index